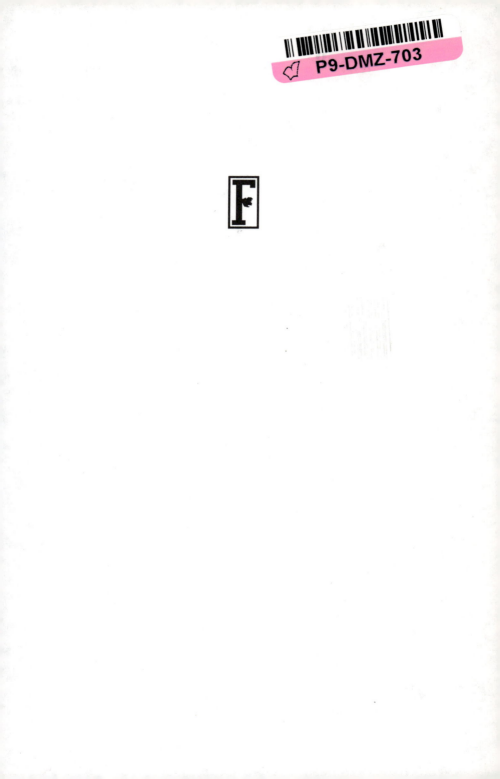

a|fireside|book

published by simon & schuster

move | your | stuff,
change | your | life

How to Use FENG SHUI
to Get Love, Money, Respect, and Happiness

by karen rauch carter

Illustrated by KAREN RAUCH CARTER
and JEFF FESSLER

FIRESIDE
Rockefeller Center
1230 Avenue of the Americas
New York, NY 10020

FIRESIDE and colophon are registered trademarks
of Simon & Schuster, Inc.

DESIGNED BY JUDITH STAGNITTO ABBATE/
ABBATE DESIGN

Manufactured in the United States of America

2   4   6   8   10   9   7   5   3   1

Library of Congress Cataloging-in-Publication Data
Carter, Karen Rauch, 1960–
Move your stuff, change your life : how to use feng shui to
get love, money, respect, and happiness / Karen Rauch
Carter ; illustrated by Karen Rauch Carter and Jeff Fessler.
    p.   cm.
    "A Fireside book."
    1. Feng-shui.   I. Title.
    BF1779.F4C37   2000
133.3'337—dc21   99-35705
                                               CIP

ISBN 0-684-86604-8 (pbk.)

acknowledgments

My special thanks to:

Professor Lin Yun, for all his wisdom

Nate Batoon, who has been kind and generous enough to teach me about feng shui and allow me to use so many of his stories for this book

Bridget Skinner, Vicki Allinson, and all the members of the Orange County Feng Shui Guild, for their support

Obie Wade, for his undying support and our conversations about what's possible

Marcela Landres, for recognizing the need for this type of feng shui book, and for her enthusiasm and editing savvy

Jeff Fessler, for helping me illustrate this book and for sharing his gift of humor

Donna Allen, Erika and Alton Burkhalter, Nancy Finley, Alison and David Hahn, Annemarie Hall, Melissa Moore, Margaret Rauch, Nancie Vollmer, and Rich Welt, who all agreed to read drafts of this book and comment

My husband, Steve Carter, who allowed me the space in our lives to take on this endeavor

And finally, all the people whose lives were changed in such outrageous ways by feng shui that they became stories in this book

To my son, Cole,
my favorite distraction while writing this book

contents

**Chapter 3: They Like Me, They Really, Really Like Me—
Fame and Reputation   65**

Chapter 6: 911—Helpful People and Travel   128

Chapter 7: At the Intersection of Possibility and Potential—Career and Life Path   142

Chapter 8: If I Only Had a Brain—Skills and Knowledge 161

Chapter 9: How Not to Play Family Feud—Family 173

how to use this book

The best way to read this book is with pen and paper in hand. Since your notes may be around for a while, I would suggest using one of those small, nicely bound blank books worthy of sitting on your nightstand or a bookshelf in your home.

Not only will this notebook become your personal feng shui guide to happiness and fulfillment; it will serve as a written account of your "old life"—the one before knowing and using the ancient Chinese secrets of feng shui.

Be inquisitive, yet have a jovial frame of mind when reading and following the advice in this book. I attempted to write *Move Your Stuff, Change Your Life* in a lighthearted, humorous manner because love and laughter are energetically more powerful for this work than sadness or seriousness. In other words, move your stuff with a smile and you will experience faster results.

If you don't control your attitude, it controls you.

move | your | stuff,
change | your | life

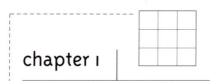

chapter 1

Opening the Feng Shui Toolbox

I f you want to create a sundae that would put Jenny Craig into a spin, you need some tools: bowl, spoon, Ben & Jerry's Chunky Monkey ice cream, and calorie-laden toppings. If you want to create a life worth living, you also need some tools: a living environment, an idea of what you want out of life, good intentions, and an understanding of the ancient Chinese secrets of feng shui (better say it right: *fung shway*). Translated, it means "wind and water."

Feng shui is just a term borrowed from the Chinese. Since they have honed this art throughout the past centuries, let's honor them by keeping their name. But don't just think of it as local Chinese wisdom—think of it as universal common sense. Everyone, regardless of culture or creed, has employed some system of thoughtful placement with regard to their living environment and furnishings. Simple spatial organization actually comes quite naturally to most humans. It's when things get complicated with contraptions like computers, microwaves, and all-terrain vehicles that mistakes are often made.

Proper feng shui is purposefully arranging the stuff around you to gain positive results. What stuff? you ask. All stuff—your worldly possessions, your desk at work, your toothbrush, your underwear. Just as that Chunky Monkey sundae affects your body when you eat it, each object you place in your living environment affects you as well. You also affect each environment you encounter. Wouldn't it be nice to know how?

This book will give you that answer. Consider it the proper nutrition guide for your home.

I want to emphasize this point a bit more because I have been asked by a few clients and friends if feng shui is a religion. Some others have asked if it can conflict with their organized religion. Although I don't claim to know the dogma of every religion, I do know that feng shui is not meant to replace or challenge anyone's religious values or ideas. It is simply a collection of environment-oriented information, just as a cookbook is a collection of food-oriented information.

If you are still questioning about this, here's a quick test to help you find your answer. If knowing how food affects your body interferes with your religion, then perhaps knowing how feng shui affects you would too. OK, 'nuff said. Let's get on with it.

Everything consisting of matter in this three-dimensional universe is placed next to something else. This spatial relationship is feng shui. So really, feng shui has been around you as long as you've been around. It is the *type* of feng shui you have around you that this book addresses. Instead of thinking everything is not feng shuied until you feng shui it, think of everything always being in some state of feng shui, and you changing it for the better.

For all you scientific minds out there, I asked Barry Gordon, a physicist as well as a feng shui practitioner, to briefly explain from a science perspective how and why feng shui works. He sees feng shui as "the intelligent use of intention through environmental metaphor." In more detail he states:

> If we accept the message of both quantum mechanics and the great spiritual teachers, then every smidgen of our universe affects every other. From this viewpoint there is no inside or outside. Everything is contained in consciousness,

which has no boundaries. So the placement of your bed has meaning in relation to the rest of your experience. The bed is a representation of your beliefs and emotions on the physical dimension, which manifest differently, and seemingly disconnected by you, on other dimensions. When your bed is moved with intention, the belief and emotion dimensions also move.

The great eighteenth-century scientist and mathematician Leibniz discovered that photons, the basic particles of light, exhibit intention and purpose. If we take light to be the whole spectrum of vibration, not only visible light, then everything is composed of photons. That means the universe is intentional. And since we have been given the ability to intend, we are co-creators of the universe that we individually experience.

Every thing, even the sticky front door that doesn't open all the way, has meaning. Every thing, every action is intentional, sometimes conscious, sometimes unconscious. Feng shui brings the unconscious in our environment back into consciousness. That brings the beliefs and feelings back into consciousness. Then we have choice and can create our universe consciously.

I don't know about you, but that's about all the science and quantum mechanics I can take in one sitting. You might want to come back to this quote after reading the book to see if it makes more sense to you. Now, let's get back to changing your life . . .

Consider this chapter the feng shui toolbox. It's not exactly the kind of toolbox that Bob Villa totes around, but it's just as important. It explains the feng shui basics: exactly what you need to know to make your dreams come true. And don't worry if you get a little spun around in this chapter. There are entire books on feng shui that attempt to explain the information I am dumping on you in Chapter I. As the rest of the book unfolds, this information is repeated in different ways, which gives you several chances to absorb the specific wisdom that is pertinent to your life and home.

Don't skip the rest of this chapter either. Although it may look enticing to skip ahead to the Prosperity or Relationship chapters, I wouldn't advise it. You wouldn't eat a sundae without the correct tools (technically, you could slurp the ice cream straight out of the carton, but that looks pathetic). So don't try to use feng shui without the correct tools.

Ch'i Wiz!

Ch'i (pronounced *chee*, like half of *cheese*) is another word for energy. Energy is what's moved around when you apply the rules of this book to your environment. By shifting the energy with cures, you can better your life. (*Cure* is just another name for balance.) You cure—balance, or enhance—something by specifically placing an item somewhere to help you in life. If you don't correct poor object placement with cures, you expend your own energy to make things happen in your life. But why waste your own energy when you can get a lamp or mirror to do the work for you? Bonus: inanimate objects don't whine about whose turn it is to expend energy.

Ba-Gwhat?

Everything that happens in life can be boiled down and placed into nine categories, or life situations. These categories are spatially represented by areas in your living quarters. Each area is called a *gua* (pronounced *gwa*). The sum of these guas put in a particular order is called the *bagua*. The *ba* of *bagua* means "eight," and the bagua has eight sides (Figure I). The eight sides plus the middle make up the nine zones that relate to the different life situations (Figure 2).

The following are the specific life situations associated with the nine zones that make up the bagua.

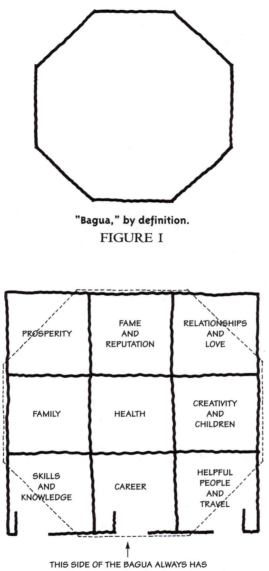

"Bagua," by definition.

FIGURE 1

Simplified bagua showing the associated life situations.

FIGURE 2

Prosperity

This area relates to wealth: having money for the good things in life (not for the necessities in life like food, rent, and phone bills). This gua is considered a power corner by many because money is seen as power, and power can get you what you want. Think Bill Gates, Donald Trump, and the person who invented Velcro. If big money is what you are looking for, work on the Prosperity corner.

Fame and Reputation

This is the area in the home that supports you as a person out in the big world. It deals with how you are perceived by others, which makes a big difference with concerns like how and where money and relationships come to you. It also has to do with your own integrity and honesty, which can make a difference in things like marriage and relationships. So, if you are a jerk, or at least people think you are, don't despair. The Fame and Reputation area can help you out.

Relationships and Love

If you are looking for a relationship, looking to make an existing one better, or simply looking for a shagedelic good time, look no further. It is vital that this part of your home be balanced so there can be harmony in relationships of all kinds. So before you give up and choose to join a cloistered convent or a group of chanting monks, check out this area.

Creativity and Children

This section of the home relates to thinking creatively. You might consider beginning with this area so you can come up with creative cures for the rest of your home. This locale is also associated with children, since children usually think creatively (like when they figure out how to put a pop tart in the disk drive of the computer). Anything to do with kids—yours, not yours, your siblings, your future kids—this is the spot to work with them.

Helpful People and Travel

This part of the home is set aside for calling upon someone who makes your life easier (easy teacher, sympathetic IRS agent, efficient waiter, the cleaning lady, truthful car dealer, networking peer). Maybe it's someone you know, or perhaps the help appears out of the blue. And of course, sometimes it's an angel from the "other side" who helps. This area is also about being treated fairly and honestly. Also, if you would like to do more or less traveling, or have a move coming up, this section applies to making these situations flow more smoothly as well.

Career and Life Path

This area of the home is linked to what you are supposed to be doing in life, whatever that is. Whether it's hard-core business, traversing a more spiritual path, or creatively mooching off others, this area of the home is dedicated to getting you on the right track in life.

Skills and Knowledge

This part of your home affects how you learn, store, and use knowledge. Although the energy in each gua will affect the other eight, this one is especially worthy of attention. For example, if you don't have the smarts to manage the money you make, it may erroneously appear that your Prosperity section is not working for you.

If you are in school, this is the area to enhance, especially if you think serious studying is when you calculate the bartender's tip on the last pitcher of Michelob.

Family

This section is associated with family issues. Montel, Jerry, Ricki, and Jenny would be out of business if everyone paid attention to this area. It also holds the energy for everyday coinage—paying for rent, food, and other necessities in life (chocolate, Chap Stick, bamboo steamers). So, if you don't have this area juiced up, your Prosperity (major coinage) area may never reach its potential.

Health and Other

The center of the bagua contains all other life situations not mentioned above. It impacts health as well. Since this area lies in the middle of the home, it touches all other areas geographically, and can literally and figuratively affect all other areas by association. As they say, if you don't have your health, you don't have anything (except doctor bills and a lot of medication that is obviously not working).

Take a moment to redraw the simplified bagua illustration (with the nine life situations inside the boxes) in your notebook. You will probably want to refer to this illustration often as you read on, and it may be easier if you have it handy in your notebook.

Although we will be discussing this information at length later in this chapter, please note the doors in the illustration. The location of the main door plays a specific role in the orientation of the bagua in a room or home.

Cures, Cures, and More Cures

Just as you eat a big, juicy Wendy's single to cure the effects of a hangover, in feng shui you *apply cures* to get what you want out of life. Remember, that's the fancy term for adding or moving stuff in the areas around your living space to balance it. There are nine categories of traditional feng shui cures. (Have you noticed a fixation with the number nine? It's a powerful number in feng shui.) These cures have been used for thousands of years to help solve problems—so much for calling feng shui a new fad. Almost without exception, you can add any of these cures to a space to help change its energy for the better. Here are the nine categories of traditional cures.

Light

By adding light to a specific area, energy is activated and will eventually foster change. Light can come from candles, electric lights, oil lamps, fires (hopefully contained within a fireplace or candle top), lava lamps, or your old Lite-Brite. This category also includes reflected light from mirrors, crystals, or shiny objects (the aluminum foil covering your sandwich or the chrome retro toaster).

Sound

Adding a pleasant sound to a space can create a change in the energy vibration and enhance your digs. Appealing sounds such as moving water, music, singing birds, chirping crickets, chimes, bells, and other musical instruments can enhance the energy of the space. Toilets flushing, belches, and gurgling garbage disposals usually don't count.

Living Things

From fish to flamingos, animals not only make great pets, they're great energy enhancers for a sluggish space. Just make sure these nonhuman companions are clean, well kept, and healthy. A Habitrail full of hamster poop not only reflects negative energy but makes your house smell like that nasty pet store in the mall. Plants are also alive with energy, provided they are actually alive. A little water and Miracle-Gro can go a long way in fulfilling your feng shui dreams.

Weight

Items that weigh a lot, or symbols of things that are heavy, are used in feng shui to ground a space. Grounding is needed when you live above the ground floor or if your head is always in the clouds. Tiny elephant statues and big boulders can both work. While a picture of John Candy or Chris Farley works, it would be in bad taste.

Color

Each area of the home corresponds to a specific color. Using the right colors in the correct area reflects positively on the person who lives there. It can be as obvious as painted walls or as subtle as colored construction paper behind a couch; as long as the color is there, it will work for you. Various colored food stains on the upholstery and carpet don't quite meet this criterion.

Moving Objects

Moving objects seem to be alive and therefore are capable of greatly energizing a space. Mobiles, chimes, water, butterfly wings, fans, and curtains blowing in the breeze are a few of the many things that exhibit these good qualities. Scampering roaches technically qualify but usually infringe upon dinner parties and make guests expend all their energy running from them.

Electric Power

Your TV, computer, alarm clock, vibrator, and automatic potato peeler are charged with electricity. So make them and all other electrical appliances work to your benefit by placing them in appropriate spots in the home. Use caution, though, when planning the location of vibrators or other sex toys (see Chapter 4).

Symbolic Objects

This category includes intentionally placing items in the home that have symbolic meaning in order to shift the energy. One symbolic traditional-cure example is a bamboo flute. Flutes can be used as a ch'i uplifter and enhancer in certain circumstances. At one time they were a symbol of the coming of good news. Today's equivalent might be things like church bells, a trumpet, a wedding invitation, or a doorbell. Although bamboo flutes don't usually fit into Western decor, feel free to use them in settings where you feel comfortable. Or if you want to fool your guests into thinking you're some hot bamboo flute musician, leave them lying around in prominent places.

Other

This category has the potential to be the most powerful, even more than Wonder Woman and Madonna combined. It is the category of cures that encompasses all other possibilities for creating a nurturing environment. The cures in this category should be personalized and have great significance to you, either symbolically or literally. *Move Your Stuff, Change Your Life* concentrates on this category and explores some unique situations and cures. You can either follow an example of what someone else has done before or be a rebel and follow your heart by doing something uniquely suited to you. After reading this book, you will know the difference and realize the power behind both options.

So Much to Do and So Little Time

Are you ready to start? Then the first step is to decide which guas get top priority.

For a good indicator of what needs most work in your home, honestly evaluate what is going on in your life—and the lives of those who live with you. Your environment is what supports you, either weakly or strongly. Either way, it definitely affects you. Ideally everyone who inhabits the home should be involved in the process, but if that is not possible, simply keep them in your awareness as you proceed. They may snicker as you put strange items behind the couch and microwave, but I promise you'll have the last laugh.

Truth or Dare

Here's an exercise to help you assess your life and guide you to where you might focus your feng shui energy.

Get out your notebook and start thinking about your life.

Are you satisfied with your career? Is that assistant managerial position at Beauford's Video and Bait Store challenging and stimulating enough for you? Do you just barely make rent each month? Ever heard the words *savings account?* Stuck in a dating rut or a boring marriage?

In your notebook, write down anything that's bothering you or coming between you and true happiness. Categories will become evident eventually, so don't worry about that now. Just keep writing, and know that they will be tended to later on in this process.

If you are having trouble being thorough, carry a paper and pen with you at all times (but no pocket protector, please). Every time *anything* bothers you, and you hear a complaint of some sort running through your head, write it down. It could be as simple as "I have a stomachache" or as complex as "My boyfriend never listens to me." Even if you are being repetitive, write down the complaint each time. You may notice a pattern of complaints or a repetitive complaint that you didn't even know you had. The following questionnaire may help you start to uncover some of your complaints.

Career and Life Path

Are you fulfilled in your current career? If not, what is it about the career that is less than optimal? People? Money? The type of work? Location? Traveling? Late nights? Stress? Lecherous boss? Boss not lecherous enough?

Skills and Knowledge

Are you content with your current level of education? Having a hard time in school? Seem to repetitively make bad decisions and wish you were wiser? Want to change careers but don't have the skills to master your dream? Feel like an idiot when you watch *Jeopardy!?* Rely on *Entertainment Tonight* for your hard news?

Family

Do you have a good relationship with your family? Wish to be treated like one of the family even when you're not a part of the bloodline? Want to start a family? Is it hard making enough money just to pay for the basics? Have they ever based an after-school special on your family?

Prosperity

Do you live paycheck to paycheck? Do you have a yearning for a material item but the main ingredient stopping you is lack of money? Make a fair sum of money but it goes out as fast as it comes in? Would you buy a pair of Ferragamo Salvatore shoes in lieu of a month's supply of groceries?

Fame and Reputation

Does it appear that people are talking poorly about you in public, hurting your career, family, or feelings? Want the courage to do something you can't seem to make yourself do? Does fear stop you from fulfilling dreams and being happy? Have you received a phone call from someone who got your number from the bathroom wall?

Relationships and Love

Are you content and fulfilled with current relationships (family, spouse, business associates, children, friends)? Feel depleted from your relationships with certain people? Wish to be in a committed relationship but can't seem to find the right person? Need an exorcist to fight off the partners you attract?

Creativity and Children

Are you having trouble having children? Having trouble with your children? Are the children leaving home too early or too late? Wish you were more creative? Burnt out or bored in your work, hobby, or life? Feel limited, as if there is no opportunity? Is switching shampoos the most creative thing you have done lately?

Helpful People and Travel

Do you always do everything yourself? Have a hard time finding the right person to help with things such as baby-sitting, home improvements, spiritual guidance, health issues, business ventures? Travel too much or too little for your liking? Do you get taken frequently or played the fool? Have a permanent *Kick Me* sign stuck to your back?

Health and Other

Do you have any complaints about your current state of health or the health of someone else living with you in your home? Find yourself eating Ho-Hos and drinking Yoo-Hoo while you ride the exercise bike? Always seem to be the first to catch the latest strain of flu going around? Think you should be happy but can't find your funny bone anywhere? Is Clutter or Pack Rat your middle name? Have any other complaints that did not seem to fit in any of the above categories?

Also, take a quick inventory of what *is* working. Get the total picture. You may just find the properly placed stuff in your home. Refer back to this list later on to see if your feng shui is working for you. Sometimes a shift can go unnoticed, because some people tend to forget the troubled times. Keep extensive notes on how things are at the start so you can laugh at those bad times when they are gone.

Once you feel comfortable with your lists, you may want to prioritize the items on the "What's Not Working" list, starting with the ones you feel need immediate balancing (for example, "I want a meaningful relationship"), and ending with items that are less of a priority (such as "I want better shoes"). This will help you choose which items to implement now, and which later, if there are cost concerns.

List the nine life situations in your notebook, and then place each complaint from the life inventory in one of the nine categories. The nine areas, once again, are (1) Prosperity, (2) Fame and Reputation, (3) Relationships and Love, (4) Creativity and Children, (5) Helpful People and Travel, (6) Career, (7) Skills and Knowledge, (8) Family, and (9) Health and Other.

Sometimes a problem falls into several categories. For example, if you are having trouble in school, you may want to place that complaint both in the Skills and Knowledge area (for obvious reasons) and in the Helpful People area (for tutors, reasonable teachers, smart friends, and Mr. Cliff and his notes). Every gua could have a complaint in it, or perhaps just a few do. The list now becomes an easy reference pointing to the problem places in your home.

This exercise should make you feel empowered because now you have all the things you want to fix in your life written down in one spot. It's time to turn these misfortunes into good fortune!

> The mere fact that you have put energy into carefully evaluating your life and writing this list will start to cause change for the better immediately. So, congratulations! You have already begun the process.

Oh, Bagua

As you found out earlier, each gua is associated with a life situation. But that's not all: each gua also has its associated colors, shapes, symbols, body parts, and so on. Of the nine bagua areas, five have elements assigned to them. Study the chart on pages 38–39 for a minute to learn what symbols and elements are associated with each of the nine guas.

I know you haven't learned what most of this stuff means yet, but I wanted you to know now that there is a cheat sheet included in this book that displays the gist of *Move Your Stuff*'s information (I think every how-to book should have one!). Use this as a quick reference when applying cures later on, or to spout unique trivia to impress friends. It may appear technical and drab now, but I think you will appreciate its simplicity later.

Take a moment to color each of the nine guas of the bagua illustration in your notebook, if you want. Use the first color on the list for each gua in the chart (for example, Prosperity is purple and Relationships is pink). The rest of this information can be transferred as well, but is not totally necessary. Simply keep this little cheat sheet available to reference after reading the book.

The Cycle of Life and Your Home

If you have ever played the round-and-round "rock, paper, scissors" game, you will easily understand what I am about to explain (and you thought that games were just for kids). As you can see in the chart, the five elements used in feng shui are wood, earth, metal, fire, and water. When these five are balanced in your home, you have better balance in your life and a better

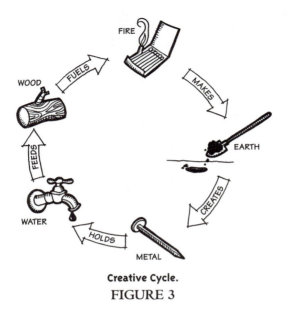

Creative Cycle.
FIGURE 3

chance to have what you want out of life. Then your home is working for you, and not the other way around. The way to use these elements is to place them in the appropriate area of the home and give intention that they work for your particular cause. Don't worry, they don't mind. They like to work.

As well as merely placing the associated element in the appropriate spot in the home, there are two additional ways to use elements. These two ways are the Creative Cycle and the Destructive Cycle. In the Creative Cycle order, one particular element creates another—water *feeds*, or creates, wood. In the Destructive Cycle order, one element overpowers another—water *douses*, or destroys, fire.

Now let's begin to apply this. In the Creative Cycle, water feeds wood, wood fuels fire, fire makes earth, earth creates metal, and finally, metal holds water (Figure 3).

Therefore (to give one example), if you want to work on getting a better reputation, having a fireplace in the Fame and Reputation gua would be a great cure, because fire is the element for Fame and Reputation. Other fire cures would be red items,

Life Situation (Bagua Area)	Element	Colors	Shape
Prosperity/Abundance		Purple, Green, Gold, and Red	
Fame/Reputation	Fire	Red	Triangular Pointed
Relationship/Marriage/ Love		Pink Red and White	
Creativity/Children	Metal	White	Round Mounded
Helpful People/Travel		Gray Black White	
Career/Life Path	Water	Black	Undulating Free-Form
Skills and Knowledge/ Wisdom		Blue Black and Green	
Family	Wood	Green	Rectangular Columnar, Vertical
Health and All Other Situations (Center)	Earth	Yellow and Earth Tones	Square Horizontal Flat

Creative Cycle Items	Destructive Cycle Items	Body Part	Associated Number
		Hip	8
Wood Green Columnar	Water Black Undulating	Eye	1
		All Major Organs of the Body	2
Earth Yellow Flat or Square	Fire Red Pointed	Mouth	3
		Head	5
Metal White Round	Earth Yellow Flat or Square	Ear	6
		Hand	7
Water Black Undulating	Metal White Round	Foot	4
Fire Red Pointed	Wood Green Columnar	Other Body Parts Not Mentioned Above	9

objects such as candles, triangular items, and those many boxes of wooden matches you may have lifted from restaurants.

If it is not practical or desirable to have a fireplace or other fire symbols there, you can use the element in the Creative Cycle that *feeds* fire: wood. Use either actual wood, such as furniture or picture frames, or a symbol of wood, like a picture of a forest or of George Washington's teeth. So remember, if you do not wish to place items in the space that directly relate to its element, try to place the element that creates it there.

Now, let's say (for example) you are in love with your white-walled, white-carpeted, and white-furnished home and want to keep it that way. From a feng shui standpoint, this would be considered very *metal* (which probably would suit Metallica fans). Why? Because white is associated with the Creativity gua, which has metal as its element (once again, refer to the chart). This would energetically be out of balance. In order to create a more harmonious situation, you could use the Destructive Cycle to balance the space. Don't think of the word *destructive* as bad (that's just an old perception). Simply think of it as another potential way to understand and balance the elements.

In the Destructive Cycle, water douses fire, fire melts metal, metal cuts wood, wood pierces earth, and earth dams water (Figure 4).

In the white-walled example above, you would use symbols of the fire element because, as you can see in the Destructive Cycle, fire *melts* metal, which would lessen the energy of so much metal in one place. A fireplace or lots of candles starts to lessen the impact of the metal. If you are opposed to adding red accents or other symbols of fire in the space because of the decor, hide the symbols. Place red cloth or paper behind pictures and under the couch cushions (don't forget to look for spare change)

There is no such thing as *hiding* in feng shui. Fortunately and unfortunately, it works both ways. Just as items placed out of view work for you in feng shui, things like clutter, dust, and dirt work against you. Your entire living space—yes, even the corn-chip-encrusted couch crevices—are a part of your feng shui energy vibration.

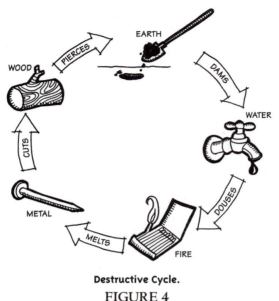

Destructive Cycle.
FIGURE 4

to get red in the space. You don't have to see it for it to work. Color vibrations know no walls.

If your head is spinning right now trying to figure all this creative and destructive stuff out, don't worry. The information is repeated several different ways throughout the book. You'll get it soon enough.

Lost in Space?

Now it's time to overlay the bagua onto your home. You can work with a blueprint or a hand drawing of your home, or simply figure things out as you walk through your home. Whichever way is easier for you to understand is best.

The goal is to divide your home into nine equal areas (no measuring necessary), like the bagua. Orient it correctly by placing the Skills and Knowledge, Career, and Helpful People edge against the wall that includes the front door.

For some, overlaying the bagua onto the home is a snap. But for some, the location of the front door is so funky, it's hard to know where to begin. When I say the front door, I am talking about the door of either the entire home or a single room within the home. The bagua can be overlaid to both. So if you live in a dorm room, rent a room, or live in an apartment, use the front door of your personal unit.

If for some reason you can't figure out which door is the formal front door, try getting in touch with your feelings for a second and use your intuition to orient the bagua. Walk up to and through each door as if you are a guest, or walk through with your eyes closed and feel if one door gives off more of a formal-front-door impression. Or try to feel which way the energy flows and the bagua seems to want to be oriented.

Look at Figure 5. In Example 1, the owner felt that the bagua should be oriented differently than the front door told him, because he knew the door was built into an old porch that had been enclosed, and that the "real" part of the house started once you entered in the door and turned right (the original location of the front door). That's how he felt the house was organized. He used the original threshold as the mouth of ch'i. As you can see, he also had an accent in the Family section. To calculate that, you measure. If the part that pokes out is less than half of the length of that whole side, it is an accent. Likewise, if a part that pokes into your home is less than half the length (see the Relationships section in Example 2), it is considered a missing piece.

The owner of the home drawn in Example 2 felt that the ch'i flowed into the home from the front to the back and oriented the bagua accordingly. With this orientation, the Relationship gua and the Helpful People gua were slightly compromised in her house.

Example 3 shows an opaque fence and gate fronting the home. Once you entered through the double-door gate, it felt as if you were in the private space of the house. In this example, you could consider the gate the mouth of ch'i and decorate the

EXAMPLE 1

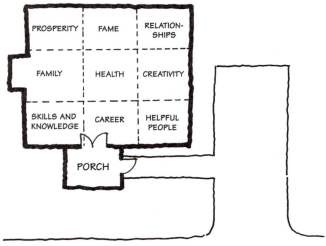

STREET

EXAMPLE 2

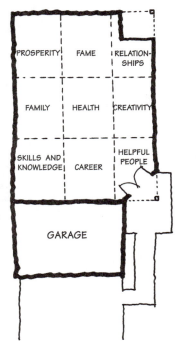

EXAMPLE 3

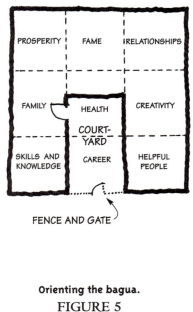

Orienting the bagua.

FIGURE 5

With a door on a 45° slant, try to intuitively feel the ch'i flow, and orient the bagua by that feeling.

courtyard appropriately as a career gua outdoor room. Declare that your home is aligned a certain way and go with it.

Remember, for the most part, the *formal front door* (the one the architect designed to be the front door) is the *main door* of the house. Even if you always enter your home through the side garage door, that would not make it the main entry—or as the Chinese describe it, the *mouth of ch'i.*

If you have found which way to orient the bagua, you are halfway there. Now all you do is go around on the main floor (the one the front door leads you into) and find the space representing each gua. The basement, second, and third floors should be taken into consideration when applying feng shui principles, but the main floor is the most important. If you live in a split-level home, try to intuitively follow the path of ch'i and apply the cures to the floor that seems most like the main floor of the home.

Calling the Panacea Police!

Feng shui can work for anyone—and work fast. But using it as a substitute for taking responsibility in your own life is certainly not recommended. You've got to do your part. The feng shui panacea police will sniff out those people who think they can simply use feng shui instead of engaging in such mundane events as doing homework in school, balancing a checkbook, or getting out from under the covers in search of a meaningful relationship. If you do your part, good old Mr. Ch'i will do his.

Got the Tools and Ain't Afraid to Use 'Em

Now you have the basic tools needed to gear up your feng shui. Although it is best to read Chapters 2 through 11 in order (especially if you are a novice), you can actually read them in any order you wish. If you are still plagued by questions—how does this work for my two-story house? how does my detached garage come into play? what do you mean by intuitively following the path of ch'i to find my way through the home?—go immediately to Chapter 11. You will find fast answers to these and other questions. Otherwise, just be sure to check out Chapter 12 when you are through with the rest of the book. It is an important chapter offering additional ways to pump up the power of your feng shui cures.

If it ain't broke, don't fix it. When you are first using feng shui, try to concentrate on fixing the problems you are currently having in your life by enhancing those specific bagua areas rather than making drastic changes in all areas. There's plenty of time to refine your feng shui after initial changes start to bring you more into balance.

chapter 2

Show Me the Money!—Prosperity

ncient Chinese secrets used properly in the Prosperity area of your home could create the following changes in your life. You could

- get a raise
- receive unexpected money
- make more money with your business
- have money to go on a dream vacation
- easily become philanthropic
- acquire a stable income
- increase wealth for the good things in life
- find inner peace and true happiness with what you have in life

It's true, there are those who were born with a silver spoon in their mouths and those who can't find enough to eat. What's with that? There are also those who win a thousand dollars in the lottery and scream, "We're rich!" and those who consider a thousand dollars loose change. Why do some people feel wealthy with ten bucks and others feel poor with millions? Answer: attitude, baby. Prosperity is a state of mind. That said, let's try to get you to a place of prosperity and abundance.

Endless supply is the first rule of the universe. You can have everything you want without robbing another in the process (what do you think of that, Robin Hood?). Yes, I'm talking about having your cake *and* eating it too. If you do not have abundance in all areas of your life, you have bought into a *lacking* state of mind somewhere along the way. By moving some stuff in the Prosperity corner, you can slowly rid yourself of that false mind-set and start to live abundantly. From now on just think of yourself as one of the Jeffersons—*movin' on up.*

Let's not get all caught up on just the money and the material side of things. Abundance is possible in more arenas than just that. Striking a balance in abundance is necessary in all parts of life. The phrase "Money can't buy happiness" summarizes the idea perfectly. Yes, money does make life easier, and yes, we are trying to achieve that with feng shui, but don't forget the bigger picture. Feeling that there is abundance in your life puts you in balance with the universe and how it is meant to be—like the abundance of the Garden of Eden, so to speak.

The first step toward the garden is actually inside the house. From just inside the front door, walk to the back left corner of the room or home. (See Figure 6. When I say corner, I'm speaking of the whole one-ninth of the home defining the Prosperity gua, not just the exact corner. There is no need for exact measurements. Each of the nine areas blends gracefully into others like the colors of the rainbow.)

What do you see? An oil-stained, cluttered garage—or an ornate armoire filled with luxurious linens? Are you surprised by what you find when you associate this corner with abundance? A long-time financially suffering friend of mine laughed when she saw that her Prosperity corner was the corner that *always leaked* when it rained. Her money was always leaking out away from her. Sometimes feng shui answers are quite literal.

Is this corner outside the house because the shape of the room or home was designed to have this piece missing (as in

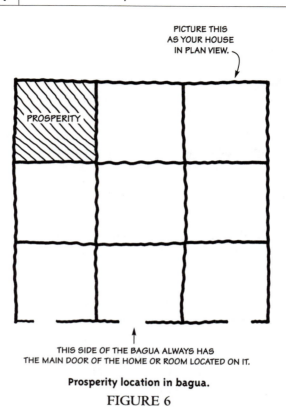

PICTURE THIS
AS YOUR HOUSE
IN PLAN VIEW.

PROSPERITY

THIS SIDE OF THE BAGUA ALWAYS HAS
THE MAIN DOOR OF THE HOME OR ROOM LOCATED ON IT.

Prosperity location in bagua.

FIGURE 6

Figure 7)? If this or any other corner of your room or home is missing, complete it by employing one of the cures for missing pieces. (Skip ahead to Chapter 11 if you want immediate cures for this situation. If not, just make a note that you need one here—you'll definitely learn about it later.)

For now, let's assume you actually have a regular and complete corner to work with. Here are some of the best items to place in the Prosperity corner. Use one, all, or however many work with your decor. "If one is good, more is better" isn't necessarily true when you use intention to create feng shui power. (You'll learn more about adding *intention power* as we go along.)

PROSPERITY	FAME AND REPUTATION	RELATIONSHIPS
FAMILY	HEALTH	CREATIVITY AND CHILDREN
SKILLS AND KNOWLEDGE	CAREER	HELPFUL PEOPLE

MAIN DOOR

Plan view of house or apartment with most of the Prosperity gua and some of the Family gua missing.

FIGURE 7

Power Tools for Prosperity

Purple   Purple is the best color for the Prosperity corner. Put a big chunk of purple amethyst there and look out! Dig out and fire up that purple lava lamp and watch the money start to ooze up and bubble over into your life. Dare I say it? Make sure Barney's place is in the Prosperity corner of your child's room.

Red   The powerful color of red can add excitement and energy to almost anything. For centuries the Chinese and many other cultures have thought that red is a very powerful color. Because of this constant thought pattern over such a very long time, red now is a very powerful color, strongly set in the universe. Remember, energy follows thought. So keep that red power tie here.

Green   Anything green will do. Just remember—use green to get out of the red. I have seen Americans use sheets of real, uncut dollar bills in frames for their potent green symbol. So if your money is green, red, or purple—use it!

> You can use the colors from either side of the Prosperity gua to achieve greater power. For example, red and green are good in the Prosperity gua because they are the colors of the neighboring Family and Fame sections.

Gold   For obvious reasons, gold stuff enhances the wealth area. Give your corner the Midas touch. Use a symbol from your heritage if you want. For example, if you are Irish, get that "pot o' gold" thing going using (chocolate) gold coins.

Symbols That Remind You of Wealth and Abundance   Change sorters and piggy banks are meaningful to some. Exotic fruits or perfumes mean wealth to others.

Another word for this area of the home is *blessings.* This is a great place to acknowledge what you have been blessed with already—your spouse, a second home, vacation photos.

Place photos of your dream car (boat, house, vacation, wardrobe) in this gua if thinking about it makes you feel abundant. Don't forget the less materialistic things like kids, pets, religious objects. Place the item, photo, or symbol of it in this corner so whenever you see it, you think of your ever growing abundance.

Moving Water   Get the cash flowing with moving water—guppies in a glass, or a raging waterfall. Just make sure the water is clean and it isn't the toilet. And if you don't have time, room, or money to get real moving water, that National Parks calendar photo of Ol' Faithful will do.

Round-Leaved Plants   A jade plant or African violet—really just about any plant—will get the energy going for you. Just remember to keep them friendly (no barrel cactus) and healthy (no plant hospitals in this corner).

Moving Objects   This traditional category of cures works well here to get money moving around you. Battery-operated kinetic decor can be the perfect answer for getting the universe to notice your needs.

Now is a good time to list in your notebook the power tools for Prosperity that you already own.

If you want big money for the good things in life, the Prosperity section of your home is where to get it. On the other hand, if you need money to get out of the hole or to pay off bills before having anything for "the good life," be sure to adjust your Family section as well. The Family section will help you acquire basic maintenance money so you can then focus on the good stuff (see Chapter 9).

Hazardous Materials for Prosperity

Now here is the list of the stuff to avoid, or stuff to counterbalance with a cure, in the Prosperity gua.

Dirt and Dust   This is not the way to attract "old money." Keep this corner orderly and clean—even if this corner falls in the garage or mudroom.

Broken Items   If it's broke, you're broke.

Reminders of Broke or Bad Times   Chuck the old-college-days photo that brings up memories of how you always had to give plasma to buy books. Also, if your kitchen cabinets or your refrigerator is near this spot, make sure you don't have Old Mother Hubbard's empty cupboards going on for you. If you can identify with Mrs. Hubbard, here are a few ideas: (1) Take some bills (either real or realistic looking), roll them up, and place them in the refrigerator or freezer. Then you will always have "cold cash" whenever you need it. (2) Buy some luxury item, like a bottle of champagne or a jar of caviar, and place it in the refrigerator. Nothing says "prosperous" like a jar of fish eggs and bubbly! But seriously, do try to stock up a little on the grub.

Trash Cans   Just don't do it.

OK, if you just have to have one there, use one with a lid. Or place a red line around the rim of the can with paint, tape, or fingernail polish. This will stop your ch'i from ending up at the local landfill.

Dead Plants I bring this up to make the point specifically about dried flowers. They are not welcome here, as they give off dead energy—something unfit for Prosperity corners.

Fireplaces A fireplace may give the suggestion that you burn through money, or else it is going up in smoke. If you have a fireplace here, balance it out by adding water, the color black, or a mirror over the mantel (mirrors equal water in feng shui). Water will mix with the fire and create steam. Steam equals power. (You'll soon find out, in upcoming chapters, the many nuances of using a mirror over a fireplace.)

Toilets Let's hope there isn't a toilet in your Prosperity corner—it can suck the cash out of your wallet like nothing else. If there is, try to place ch'i-uplifting items in the bathroom. Use as many power tools from the above list as you can without cluttering the space. Use mirrors all the way around the room, or at least two mirrors facing each other in the bathroom. Or get a few small ones and place them either on the floor behind the toilet, or in the tank, or on the countertop near the corner. Make sure they are all facing up. Another way to deal with the situation is to place eye-catching pictures high up so everyone who goes into the bathroom looks up. (If no signs of improvement occur, it may be time to call in a professional feng shui consultant.)

Regarding plumbing fixtures: Keep toilet lids closed when they are not in use. Close drains in sinks and tubs, too. Another ch'i-saving secret is to place a red ribbon or red tape around the outgoing pipes of your plumbing (sink, toilet, bathtub drain) to stop the ch'i from going "down the drain." (More on drains in Chapter 6.)

Using Rags to Get Riches

How do you use rags to get riches? It all starts with a clear intention to receive more money. Picture it: *money*—a specific amount. And don't sell yourself short. Get enough to cover everything. It helps me if I write the number down; so go ahead, grab a pen, write a sum down . . .

What went on in your mind as you wrote it? Did you say, "Yea, right," as if you doubted it? Or did you daydream of all the things you did and bought with the money? Well, I can guarantee, the latter has more feng shui power. It is *all in your head— and feelings.* And placing this list and the other things listed as power tools for Prosperity in the gua helps your head remember what you asked for. So, get moving that stuff now!

Where do you start? First, make sure the space is clean. The last thing you want in your Prosperity area is cobwebs and dust. If that treadmill that currently doubles as a valet is there, it's time to lose it. You don't want any reminders of unfinished business here. (If you swear you are going to get back into using it, at least move it to the Health or Creativity section.)

Next, start placing the power tools. The color purple is the color associated with the Prosperity area. So, the more purple you can place there, the better. Dye the curtains, change the bedding, paint the walls, line the drawers! If it looks good, do it. Use purple dust rags to clean the house, to remind yourself that you are keeping things clean for abundance. If your closet is in this corner, start wearing more purple and fill your closet with purple clothes. If your office is there, use purple files in your drawers.

> Remember, feng shui adjustments can work where no one actually sees them. If your Prosperity corner, with purple in it, would rate high on the ugly chart, try to find a place to hide the color. Purple shelf paper in drawers, purple construction paper behind pictures or under furniture, and purple paint on a concrete floor before carpeting is laid will all work, even though they are hidden away.

Using Riches to Get Out of Rags

Next, place some items in the area that remind you of wealth: rare coins, a full piggy bank, the Boardwalk and Park Place game pieces from the Monopoly game, pictures of jewels. Whatever it is, create a space for these items and take special care for them, because they are taking care of you.

My friend Twila loves nice jewelry. She created a treasure chest out of her jewelry box in her Prosperity area closet. She had the little chest always spilling pearls and jewels, and she pretended that they were all real and priceless. Even though I usually preach keeping things organized and orderly, I thought her overflowing chest was the perfect enhancement for her.

The stove is considered a Prosperity element in the home wherever it is. The number of burners is also important—more are better. The reason goes back to China: if you can cook for many people at once, you must have the money to buy a lot of food. Therefore, the more burners, the more wealth there must be in the home. Make sure all the burners work and that the stove is kept clean at all times. Place a reflective material (mirror, Mylar) behind the stove to symbolically double the quantity of burners. You can place a shiny teapot or pan on the stove to reflect them as well. Tip for young girls: shine up that Easy Bake Oven and place it in the Prosperity corner of your bedroom if you are looking for a raise in allowance!

If cash is what you are looking for, then maybe cash is what you should place in this corner. Try this magic money cure: take nine consecutively numbered dollar bills (or whatever paper money you use), laminate them and make a mobile from them, and hang it in the Prosperity corner. A more subtle way is to fan nine dollar bills out and place them in the corner behind furniture. Watch the money flow!

My home office happens to be in the Prosperity corner of the house. Besides writing books and practicing feng shui, I am also a landscape architect and site planner. I juiced up the corner with just about everything. I have a bamboo flute (traditional ch'i enhancer) resting on top of a chunk of purple amethyst. I also have a wind chime hanging in the skylight, which is just above a map of the world. (I intended money to come from all around the world!) After a while, I was scouted out by some developers in the Middle East to do some work for them. They had never met me before but insisted I was the one to site-plan their land parcels in Marbella, Spain, and Jiddah, Saudi Arabia. "Little ol' home office me?" I thought—of all the people in the world with big staffs and offices, why me? Then, as I was looking up Jiddah on that world map, I noticed that it was directly below the wind chime. Like a beacon, my chime was guiding a source of prosperity directly to me.

Is This the Stairway to Heaven, or Hell?

For some reason it seems this little feng shui tip is already well known, but to be thorough, I'm going to mention it anyway because it deals with money. If the bottom step of the staircase to the second floor faces a main door into the house, the ch'i, symbolizing your money, can roll right out. (Yes, you may have left the Prosperity corner for a moment, but please bear with me.)

Here are a couple of cures to use if you are faced with this staircase alignment. Either hang a multifaceted glass crystal between the bottom step and the door, with the intention of dispersing the ch'i, or place red (like a red line or floor mat) at the bottom of the stairway, with the intention of stopping the ch'i. Either way is pretty effective.

You also want to make people notice the main floor of the house upon entering, instead of wondering what's upstairs (this creates split intention and weakened ch'i). Place something very eye catching (like a big bunch of flowers) to the side of the staircase, so full attention is drawn to it and away from the staircase.

Credit Card Blues? Try Another Color

If that American Express bill is on its way and you have no clue where the money to pay it is coming from, you may be slightly lacking in money wisdom as well as money. The last thing you want in this lifetime is bad credit. So, as well as doing some improvements to the Prosperity section, I would suggest shining up the old wisdom area (Skills and Knowledge) as well. You don't have to think too hard to come up with people who made millions and then declared bankruptcy very soon after. Do Vanilla Ice, Hammer, and Mike Tyson ring a bell? This proves that having plenty of money still doesn't ensure financial freedom and a feeling of abundance. What's missing is the wisdom to use money properly. I always suggest making changes to the Skills and Knowledge (wisdom) section when the money starts to flow, because if you don't know how to make the money work for you, there will never be enough. Do something extra to this area with the intention that by doing it you are creating the wisdom necessary to handle the upcoming prosperity. If there is someone you respect for their wisdom, either write their name on a piece of blue paper or get a picture of them and place it in the Skills and Knowledge section of your home or room (see Chapter 8). If you can't think of anyone, perhaps a penny with Lincoln on it will do—a man admired for his intelligence, actually *on* money.

I knew of a politician who had the laundry room in his Prosperity corner—can you say "money laundering"? I say this as a reminder to read the space very literally and see what it is saying to you, and saying about you to others.

Bust a Move—There's No Place Like Your Own Home

If you are looking for money for something specific like a new home, make sure your Prosperity section knows that. Draw up a plan for your dream house, research architects and landscape architects, or cut a picture of your dream home out of a magazine. Write down, "I am now receiving money for my dream home," and place it in this corner. (By now you've already figured out that purple ink or paper is cool for this, right?) Or perhaps place the item in a purple frame and hang it in this corner. This will work for anything you need money for, not just a home. So, whatever it is, find a way to express it in the Prosperity corner.

My client Jessica decided that she no longer wanted to live in the rat race. She wanted a big home in the country. In her Prosperity corner, which was her walk-in closet, she framed her dream floor plan that she found in a magazine along with a photo she took that she called "the view from the house." Jessica hung a small wind chime above it so the "wind" of feng shui would find it.

Last time I tried to contact her, the phone number was no longer valid. I heard from a friend of hers that she had indeed moved!

As Soon As I Win the Lottery . . . Well, Here's Your Magic Ticket

Waiting to win the lottery so you can get back on your feet? Or better yet, waiting for the right person to come along to marry you and bail you out? How about that inheritance or big raise? If you are looking at external sources to fix your current financial problems, but in the meantime still spend more than you earn, you might want to rethink your Prosperity and Family areas. This cycle of feeling broke and then spending to feel better can eat away at your self-esteem. It sets up a spiraling sequence of negative events. If you want to break the cycle, here's what you need to do.

You have to want a different life bad enough. That means taking responsibility for your life and getting into the mind-set that you can change it yourself. If you clean up your own situation yourself, you will never again have to worry about money. If you rely on others to fix it, you may have to continue relying upon them. Does knowing this make you more inspired to do it yourself? Yes, it is OK to have helpful people along the way, but they should enter your life to help without your having to give up control or, worse, your self-worth.

Enhancing the Family area will aid in getting those basics in life taken care of—rent, food, and mundane bills. You know, the boring stuff. When these boring bills aren't taken care of, everything is in turmoil. Once these basics are met, then the Prosperity area takes over. It supplies money for the good things in life—vacations, better cars, bigger homes. You know, the fun and frivolous stuff.

Dirty Money

What if the Prosperity section of your house is your messy teenage son's room? Well, since this is considered a power corner, he may be enjoying having power in the household. And if he is messy, he may be counterbalancing all of the hard work you are doing in the rest of the home for Prosperity. Who really knows what a stinky pit-stained jersey in this corner might do for you? I would guess it's not good. If this is the way it must be for now, make sure the Prosperity areas of every other room in your house and on your property are in perfect order to counterbalance the temporary pigpen. (Yes, you can overlay the bagua onto your lot as well. Use the formal front of the lot as the front door side.) You might request permission to place something in the room with Prosperity intentions (like a purple piece of velvet behind the WWF poster).

No Time to Waste—Show Me the Money *Now*

While remodeling her Prosperity corner kitchen, my friend asked for feng shui advice. I suggested she add as much purple as she could. When she approached her skeptical husband with the idea, he thought we both were nuts. But somehow she prevailed. One Super Bowl Sunday, before they went partying, they painted their kitchen ceiling a beautiful shade of periwinkle. Later that day, and after the game, I received a call from them as they were coming home from the party. They had both won their office pools, totaling $400. "We're gonna paint the whole kitchen purple, baby!" the once-skeptical husband shouted. In less than eight hours, they had added to their abundance.

If that is not fast enough for you, get this: Another friend asked me about feng shui and how it could work for him. He was in between jobs and wondering not only about finances, but about what he was going to do next. Knowing his awesome talents, I couldn't believe he had any trouble getting work. Although I had never been to his house, I explained how to find the Prosperity corner of his cottage. When I asked him what was in that area, he said, "There's a rickety washing machine, an ironing board, and an overflowing kitty litter box. Why?" Naturally, being the somewhat sarcastic feng shui counselor, I said, "No wonder your finances are in such crappy shape!" I told him to clean out the cat box immediately. Then I said to get something purple and stick it up there right away. The minute he hung up the phone he cleaned the box and looked for something purple. All he had was a sort of fuchsia pink spool of wrapping ribbon. So he sat it on the washing machine and walked away thinking the problem was solved. In half an hour, the phone rang with, as he says, the most creatively challenging job offer he had received to date, not to mention the highest paying— designing an interactive theme park in Europe. He was blown away. So he immediately went to the laundry room, stripped down the curtains, and dyed them purple. He rehung them, then thoroughly cleaned, and put up a wind chime. He's been humming a new tune ever since.

Where people go, so goes ch'i. Picture the mall during the holiday season and an abandoned warehouse. Which one feels more alive with energy?

| King in a High Chair |

The Prosperity corner of your home is equal to the king's throne. At all occasions the king is meticulously placed in the most dominant position. Look at your Prosperity corner with such reverence. If this corner is in your master bedroom, you are the king. If it is a family room, kitchen, or dining room, use the above-mentioned cures and you are fine. If it is your guest bedroom, a child's room, or worse yet, your mother-in-law's quarters, you may be in for a power struggle within the home. If it is a guest room, it may be vacant some of the time. In this case, uplift the ch'i and get it moving by adding movement. Use it as a hobby room when guests are not around so family members use the space. Placing an aquarium or other permanent moving cure in the room is also a suitable solution.

On the other hand, when guests are there, they may not want to leave when originally planned. If it is the dreaded mother-in-law's room, she may assume she is in charge. If it is a child's room, they may not know their place within the family structure and may attempt to run the show. But if the child is suffering from low self-esteem, this may be the perfect balancing spot for them. Just be very careful to whom you give the power corner.

| You Get What You Give |

Some people call this philanthropy, but it is true, you reap what you sow. So, just do this—give to others. When you do, you give to yourself. This is another one of those weird universal laws that would take way too long to explain. There is a catch, though. You must give freely—no strings attached. The only words in your heart should be, "I am free to give because there is always supply for my every demand."

I am living proof that this law is true. Just before studying feng shui, I was at a point—during the recession of the early nineties (most Californians were calling it a depression)—

where I literally had one dollar to my name. I was living on borrowed time with the landlord, and buying food and gas on my few remaining credit cards. One day, as I exited off the freeway, I saw a man asking for money. Although that is not an unusual occurrence in southern California, it was unusual at this off ramp. It was in the middle of nowhere by California standards.

Since I was one dollar away from being out there with him, I thought, "What the heck—at least he has the courage to ask." I dug that bill out of my purse and gave it to him. I can still see the scene as if it happened in slow motion—my hand reaching out and connecting with his. There was an immediate shift inside me—a total surrender. It made me smile. Later that day, I received a call (thank God I bribed the phone company for more time). Someone wanted me to do some work for them. It truly was the turning point of the recession and the beginning of living abundantly for me.

If you ask for money and prepare for the possibility that you will not receive it, you will get the situation you have prepared for. So instead of tempting fate, have faith.

Checks and Balances and Ch'i, Oh My!

Another way to get the checks rolling in is to balance the Prosperity corner of your home or room with an item representing each of the five elements. Use this cure also if you have absolutely no sense of style and don't care about home decor but do want to make changes in your life. This may be just the simple shift you need to begin the process of caring about your environment. The five elements are, again, *wood, fire, earth, metal, and water.* Here's an example: a wrought iron (metal) table with a glass (water) top, holding a plant (earth), a wooden (wood) picture frame, and a candle (fire). As you progress through the rest of the book, you will get a better idea of which items best represent these elements. Even if they are small tokens of each, your efforts *will* pay off. I call this the *cover-your-butt cure.* I put this cure here in the Prosperity chapter because it happens to be the first gua treated in this book. But this cure can be used in any section of the bagua, for any life situation—use it if you have a feng shui situation that you can't figure out or because this cure speaks to you as making the most sense. It will make a difference for the better either way.

By the way, if you are worried about placing a Destructive Cycle element item in the area, don't be. When each of the five elements is equally represented as a cure, the Destructive Cycle is not created.

Opposites Attract

If you have enhanced your Prosperity area and find that results are still not what you expected or intended, take a look at the opposite gua, Helpful People and Travel (see Figure 8). Although we will be discussing this area in depth later, it needs to be brought up with regard to Prosperity. The Helpful People section provides a basis of support for you to proceed in life abundantly. If you feel supported, you have confidence. This confidence promotes generosity, which in turn makes you feel and become abundant.

In case you are wondering, yes, all opposing areas of the bagua directly relate to each other. They are the yin and yang that make the whole. Balance them both for optimal results. You will find out in Chapter 6 how to enhance the opposing gua to Prosperity—the Helpful People area of the home.

Hip to Be Square

I don't know how they came up with these body parts for each gua, but the Prosperity area of the home is associated with the hip. So if you have a hip condition, place one of the power tools in the area with the intention of helping it out. (If you're just trying to be hip, skip ahead to Chapter 8.)

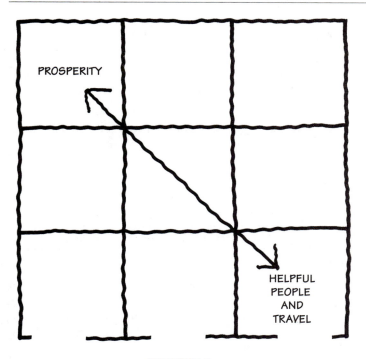

FIGURE 8

Pieces of Eight

From a numerology standpoint, the number 8 is the number for gaining material wealth. So if you live on Eighth Street, it should be easier to draw money toward you. To figure out what your address equals in numerology-speak, add up all the numbers in your address until it becomes a number between 1 and 9. For example, if you live at 24881 Flowing Creek Drive, add 2+4+8+8+1. This equals 23. Then add the 2 and 3 and you get 5. You live in a 5 house. There is a way of adding up the letters too, but for the purposes of this book, we will not be getting into such detail. Every chapter and every life situation will have its *best* and its *most challenging* number. As I said here, the best number for prosperity is 8. The most challenging is 7, which is associated with thinking more spiritually, and therefore concentrating less on material abundance. Think back to other places you have lived and remember the theme of living in those homes. Write them down and then, as you progress throughout this book, you can see what kind of luck the home's vibration offered you while you lived there. (If you are impatient and wondering about your particular number, see that chart in Chapter I.) If you have more than one home, consider the number of your primary residence as the most powerful over you.

Immediate Action Items for Prosperity

Every chapter pertaining to a gua has a list of immediate action items to remind you of any essential changes to make. Everyone can benefit from these changes—even if this particular gua is working well for you. If you do need feng shui help in this area of life, move on to balance the space using the power tools and hazardous materials information. Here are the immediate action items for Prosperity:

1. Clean this section of the home very well.
2. Remove broken items.
3. Consider calling in the pros if you have a toilet here.
4. Add enhancements as necessary.

Prosperity in Summary

Power Tools: purple, green, red, gold, things that remind you of abundance, moving water, round-leaved plants, moving objects

Hazardous Materials: dirt and dust, broken items, reminders of bad times, trash cans, dead plants, fireplaces, toilets

Opposite Gua: Helpful People and Travel

Body Part: hip

Associated Number: 8

chapter 3

They Like Me, They Really, Really Like Me—Fame and Reputation

ooking for fame? Look no further. Looking to change your reputation out there? Keep reading. You can enhance your reputation or become famous when you incorporate feng shui principles in the Fame and Reputation area of the home. And with your reputation enhanced, you may see improvement in your life in the following ways:

- ◎ Business increases or improves (translating into more money).
- ◎ You finally have the courage to do something you have always been afraid to do.
- ◎ You gain respect from your spouse, family, coworkers, friends, and strangers.
- ◎ Your good reputation is protected.
- ◎ You become very well known.
- ◎ You get the credit you finally deserve.
- ◎ You have support from others because they see you as valuable.
- ◎ You accept yourself for who you are.

First of all, even though the word fame is in the title, merely becoming famous is not what this chapter is all about. But by taking a look at famous people and dissecting the path they took to get them where they are, we start to see some common denominators regarding Fame and Reputation. People may judge you by a whole career, or simply a singular event. Lucille Ball is famous for her lifetime career achievements, and Lee Harvey Oswald is known for a one-time event. Obviously, from this example, there are two kinds of fame or notoriety—the good and the bad. Although there are some real sickos out there that would enjoy the pursuit of a bad reputation, we are going to concentrate only on how to create a good one. If you are bummed because you already have a bad reputation, this chapter will give you the tools to change it.

Being famous and having a reputation takes other people to accomplish. Simply calling yourself famous does not a famous person make. The notice or recognition of others is a vital ingredient in the recipe for both fame and having a reputation. So, how do you get other people to regard you as you wish to be regarded? First you have to choose what you want to be known for. Be very clear about it—and then *be it.* Assume you already are known for it. For example, everyone who knows me knows I am always on time. I often tell new people in my life that I am "hopelessly on time." My punctuality even relies on California freeways to get me where I need to go. I had a friend say she thought about calling the local hospitals when I actually was a little late. So, as you see, I have the reputation for being prompt. I believe that being on time shows respect for others. I also believe that you get what you give. So, by being on time, I am actually gaining respect from others.

It usually takes time to build your fame or reputation using the above method of simply "being it." If you don't have the time, use feng shui. The Fame and Reputation area of your home is located in the center of the rear wall from the main door (Figure 9). (Remember, if this area is missing, Chapter 11 has tips for completing missing pieces.)

From the chart in Chapter 1, we learned that Fame and Reputation is associated with the color red, triangular shapes, and the element of fire. With that in mind, take a further look

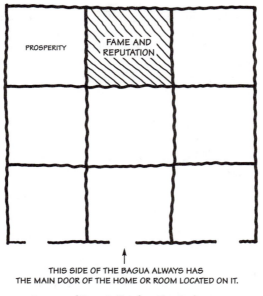

THIS SIDE OF THE BAGUA ALWAYS HAS
THE MAIN DOOR OF THE HOME OR ROOM LOCATED ON IT.

Fame and Reputation location in bagua.

FIGURE 9

at the items that may bring about a change for the better in this area.

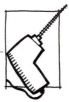

Power Tools for Fame and Reputation

Fire   Fire is the element connected to Fame and Reputation. So if you can literally add the element to the space, you are helping to build your reputation. Fireplaces, lanterns, and candles are perfect. No, they don't have to be lit all the time.

How about digging out those old photos of that trip to Hawaii and framing a montage of spewing-volcano snapshots? Lava is like solid fire. Why not use a lava lamp?

Lights   If you can't have the real thing, go for the next best. Those flickering bulbs that imitate candles or an elegant

Wherever you have a fireplace, temper it with a little water, especially if it is in the Children, Prosperity, or Family section. But even if it is in the Fame section, a little water will help balance it and actually give it power (water and fire make steam).

torchère all work well here. If you can discern between tacky and tasty, check Las Vegas out for lighting ideas. Compare the reputations with the lighting at some of these casinos and you will start to understand the connection.

Red Stuff This is *the* color for this area, so load it up. Red candles hold two desirable attributes for Fame and Reputation—the color and the element.

Since red lights have historically been used to denote districts or businesses of lower character and bad reputation, it's best to stay away from them, unless, of course, they are appropriate for your occupation.

Triangular Objects Symbolic of a fire shape, triangles and pointed objects work best in the Fame space, creating fire for the subconscious. The pink triangle eventually chosen by gays and lesbians to represent their cause and to change their perception by and reputation with others was a good choice (despite its original World War I function). Pyramids pack the perfect punch to garner respect. Cactus are dangerous feng shui items almost anywhere but here.

If you need a place in the house to display or keep collections of weapons, this is the place. Spears, harpoons, arrows, daggers, swords, and knives all have the sharp shape of fire.

Wood In the Creative Cycle, wood feeds fire. Add wood to boost the element of fire in this area, literally or symbolically. Use wooden furniture, picture frames, or treelike plants. Place the Christmas tree here and see how it changes things during the holidays.

Cheesy particleboard furniture is borderline. Woody, the cowboy character from the film *Toy Story*, is stretching it.

Green Symbolizing wood in feng shui, almost anything green will do. An avocado tree—yes. A dried and crusty bowl of guacamole from last week's build-your-own-taco party—no. *¿Ve la diferencia?*

Television Use the television as a fire symbol and place it in the Fame position (it is usually blazin' with action and movement). Don't put out the fire by channel surfing too much!

Rectangular and Columnar Objects Pictures on the wall in a vertical format, a grandfather clock, columns, or an armoire fit the bill for this section. Think of a tree trunk to remember this one.

Items That Represent Fire Gold stars, the Statue of Liberty's torch, a picture of a campfire, firefly, or volcano all work. So will a ceramic sun, a book of matches, a hibachi, incense, firecrackers, or something that survived a fire that means something to you. A string of red chili peppers can be a very effective way to spice up Fame.

Stained Glass Add red-and-green sunlight to a space by hanging stained glass in a nearby window.

Animals and Things Made from Animals Leather, wool, and eel skin are some choices that have the right energy. Live animals are great too. They are said to have fire energy. Stick the scratch pole here to entice the cats. The wooden bookcase holding the red leather-bound books is perfect. Pictures of animals are fine, but be careful on this one—the animal you choose may symbolically represent you to others. So, if you don't think of yourself as a tiger, leave Tony on the cereal box. And if you don't want to be mousy, a weasel, a snake, or bullheaded, well, you get it. This rule applies to nonanimal items as well—if it is not you, it may give mixed signals.

Plants Plants have wonderful energy for Fame. As the plant grows, so does your reputation.

Pictures or Memorabilia of Celebrities or People You Admire
If they have a reputation you want, put their stuff there.

Recognition Items Awards, diplomas, professional licenses, 4-H ribbons, gold stars on good papers, report cards, Oscars, Emmys, certificates of appreciation from local organizations can all be placed here to build your image. They will toot your horn so you don't have to.

Personal Wish List Write on a red piece of paper everything you wish to gain from enhancing this gua and safely place it somewhere in this part of the home. Write whatever you want the public to think about you.

"Up" Stuff Stuff associated with height—mountains (especially tall, pointy ones like volcanos), birds, balloons, stars, moon, sun, and other things that you usually have to look up to see—work well for a good reputation and getting people to look up to you.

Real Mountains If you live somewhere on a hillside with a big mountain out your back door, you've got about all you need for this gua. Mountains give stability to fire.

Don't forget to add some of these ideas to your notebook. Also, look around for hazardous materials that need to be moved and be sure to note them.

Hazardous Materials for Fame and Reputation

Water Water douses fire in feng shui. It's best not to have too much of it here. If your bathtub, shower, or toilet is here, balance the space using the Creative and Destructive Cycles. An example is to place earth (potted plants in ceramic pots) in the room. This can help balance out the water. How about a yellow soap on a rope for the shower? Unless you are a marine biologist or reef diver, move the fish tank. And unless you are Mark Spitz or Greg Louganis, or have an overriding cure, a pool is not the greatest item to have located near this spot of the home. My suggestion is, if the water is movable, move it. We'll deal with nonmovable water later. I'm also talking about both literal water and symbols of it. A giant painting of an ocean scene is not doing anyone much good around here.

Black Stuff   The color black symbolizes water, so get it out of here. If that little black book hasn't done enough damage yet, it will here.

Things That Symbolize What You are *Not* About   A poster of Darth Vader, a sad clown, art that includes slain animals and people, or photos of infamous people can really bring your reputation down. Also, pictures of animals associated with negative traits or water, like leeches, sharks (unless you are a mean-ass attorney), pigs, toads, piranhas, rats, or mice (we'll let Mickey slide here if you are in the themed-entertainment industry), can give a bad impression as well.

Mirrors   Since mirrors equal water, try to clear big ones out of this area, especially if you have one hanging over the fireplace. Although it is appropriate to have a little water, don't overdo it and completely put out the fire with a mirror that's bigger than the fireplace. Trust your instincts to know when it's too much.

If you have family photos resting on the mantel, make sure they are protected with a little water (especially if they are children's pictures). Without protection, people may be prone to fevers or, at a minimum, heated discussions, due to their proximity to fire. One method is to place the photos on a black background within the frame or place black on the back of the frames.

Swimming in Fame

If you are lucky enough to have a home on the beach but are now freaked about having the entire ocean in your Fame and Reputation gua, here is what you can do about that. Place elements of earth throughout and around the house, such as stone, boulders, or actual earth with potted plants. Also use elements of fire (which creates earth), such as candles or fire pits.

I know we're talking about stuff outside the home right now, but I see this condition often enough to mention it. If it's a big fat pool in your backyard soaking up your reputation, surround it with potted plants. Nine plants in red ceramic pots work well because nine is a great feng shui cure quantity. Or use lush shrubbery and trees in the area (Figure 10). Boulders in the landscape can also help the balance.

Did you ever notice on TV that rich crooks, bad guys, and womanizers are usually depicted in contemporary homes with big, hard-angled pools in back, and these pools have absolutely

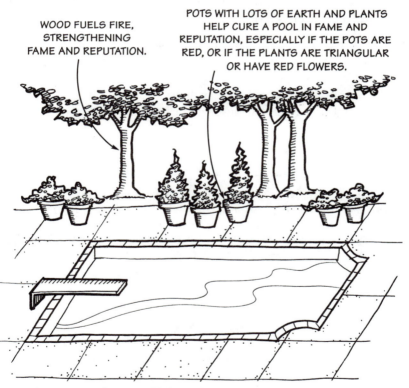

WOOD FUELS FIRE, STRENGTHENING FAME AND REPUTATION.

POTS WITH LOTS OF EARTH AND PLANTS HELP CURE A POOL IN FAME AND REPUTATION, ESPECIALLY IF THE POTS ARE RED, OR IF THE PLANTS ARE TRIANGULAR OR HAVE RED FLOWERS.

Cures to use when a pool is located in the Fame and Reputation gua.

FIGURE 10

nothing around them? And that happy people and nice families always have soft-edged pools surrounded by trees and lush landscaping? From a feng shui point of view, the pool with nothing around it is out of balance in the rear of the house. A stark pool in the Fame area of the yard can lead to questionable ethics and integrity. Be careful if you are doing business with someone living with this situation—they may be tempted to cheat or make bad decisions. If you don't want plants hanging around your pool, perhaps use red or green towels or chaise cushions. Make sure you enhance the Skills and Knowledge area extensively, though (Chapter 8), so you will have the wisdom to do the right thing in life. Also, enhance the Fame and Reputation areas of the home and each room comprehensively for added balance.

Undo a "Dis"—Get Respect

Girls, are you wondering why you never get taken home to meet your boyfriend's mom? Guys, do you get the "dis" handwave from your partner after trying to communicate your opinions? If you had respect from others, such frustrating events should not be in your life.

Everybody needs and wants respect. It goes hand in hand with everything else you do in life: your business, your love life, your relationships with friends, coworkers, and family. Respect is essential in creating a good reputation—Aretha Franklin really knew her stuff.

If you have been "dissed" by someone, you need to either gain their respect or regain ground you've lost with them. Fear not, it is quite simple. Start by going to your Fame and Reputation area. Take a look at it with your feng shui eyes (and the above list of power tools and hazardous materials). Check for obvious violations—swimming pool, spa, bathtub, or fish tank. Then tune into the more subtle ones—a world map that displays all of the earth's oceans, or a calendar of waterfalls.

If you don't have any major atrocities in the Fame section but still got dissed, you may want to do a simple intention cure.

Write the word RESPECT on a piece of red paper and place it in the area with the intention that everyone in your life respect you. If you are looking for respect from a specific person, write, "I receive total respect from _____," on the piece of paper and place it in the Fame section of the house or your bedroom. Each effort you make with the intention of gaining respect will help you to never be dissed again.

If you don't like the paper idea but still want respect from a certain someone, place a cactus or a thorny rose here for the same result. I like the rose, personally, because it says, "I am nice and beautiful, but don't mishandle me or you might get hurt." Pick which one you like best.

Fame Is Not a Four-Letter Word

If being in the spotlight is your dream and you literally want to become famous, here's my advice for you. Start by clearing all items in the Fame section that have a connotation of something that doesn't represent who you want to be. Then you can start the fun with your quest for fame.

Here is an example: If you want to be known on TV, then draw a television front on some poster board, cut away the part where the screen is, and stick the TV front to a mirror you use every day, so when you look in the mirror, you are in the television. Do this for twenty-seven days. Each time you look into it say the affirmation "I am a well-known _____ (actress, host, newscaster, commentator) on television and it fulfills me in my life path," or any other affirmation that suits you. Or paste your photo on the front of the *TV Guide* and throw it on the coffee table for a while. Try it for nine or twenty-seven days (once again, those good feng shui quantities). As you continually stumble onto it you will probably go from finding it funny to eventually becoming complacent with it. Try to get to a place where you are comfortable with the idea of seeing your face on the cover of such a magazine. The more you can picture it and daydream about it, the more energy you are putting toward it.

A much simpler cure is to place a head shot or photo of yourself on top of the TV or in the entertainment center.

The Red Carpet Treatment

I knew of one guy in Hollywood who took everything regarding feng shui to the extreme. He was a director and yearned to be famous in the industry. It just happened that a guest bathroom was in his Fame area. When he found out that red was the color for Fame, he immediately went to work. He had the toilet changed to a red one, painted the walls, floor, door, and ceiling red, and replaced all the decorative furnishings with red ones. And in true Hollywood fashion, he placed a long red carpet on the floor. Oh, he became famous all right—as the weird guy in Hollywood with the red bathroom!

I use this example to demonstrate the importance of balance with feng shui. The red bathroom had become a sign of desperation—as if the fellow believed he couldn't ever become famous on his own merit. He thought he needed some outside sources to deliver his fame and wasn't taking responsibility for it. He did not make the internal shift within. When enhancing the Fame area with balance, he should have had the confidence that his request for fame had been heard and was surely on its way with much less red.

Don't confuse self-worth with net worth.

"Hello, I Do Exist!"

Are you tired of other people getting the credit you deserve? About fifteen years ago, I contributed significantly in the designing and development of a jazz festival that has become a yearly event ever since. Heck, I even named it. At the volunteer celebration, someone else was given all the credit and accolades. Did I pipe up and say something? No. I remained the doormat and waited for someone else to come along and step on me. When I now consider where I lived and what was in the Fame area of my home, I have to laugh—a big black dining table! It all made perfect sense. With all that *water* putting out my fire in my Fame area, it's no wonder no one noticed me. Now the Fame area of my home says, "Hello, I do exist!" with plenty of red, a copy of this book, and a newspaper article about feng shui that quoted me.

Be on the lookout for thieves of Fame. Make sure you do not have any unbalanced hazardous materials in this area.

Building a Reputation One Block at a Time

My client Maggie is looking to start a career in music as a singer. She has no formal training or real connections in the industry, but I believe she will succeed in her quest because of her very deliberate and balanced approach to feng shui.

I counseled Maggie on what symbols mean in feng shui terms and asked her to empower herself by creating her own cures. I told her that the more intention, feeling, and visualization she could attach to her cures, the faster they would work. She immediately went about creating her unique Fame area. First, she dug out her box of old 45s, which symbolized her introduction to music. The Doors' "Light My Fire" was the record she chose to represent her love of music, because the word *fire* was on it (the element for this area) and because the label was red. Next she sifted through some sheet music and decided that two songs represented her feelings toward her upcoming future in music: "The Stuff That Dreams Are Made Of" by Carly Simon and Sarah McLachlan's "Building a Mystery." She then proceeded to carefully frame the single and the sheet music on a burgundy background, inside a red wooden frame.

Maggie also decided to create a benefit concert for pediatric AIDS. She is currently fund-raising for this concert. The concert is already helping her by being the subject of conversation when she cold-calls people in the music industry. She is building respect, a good reputation, and valuable relationships by attaching herself to this charity event. So when people think of her, they will think of a generous person. People seem naturally drawn to those they think are generous. I don't think she realizes it, but she has created the perfect *giving-to-receive* cure.

Glowing Reviews

What if you are interviewing for a job and you find yourself equally qualified with another person? Who is going to get the job? The one with the better Fame and Reputation area, that's who. If you have given intention to your placement of objects in this area of the home, it will help you shine a little brighter on a subconscious level—which is just the thing that is needed in situations like this. As an added boost, place the interviewer's name (if you know it) in the Helpful People corner (see Chapter 6).

The Red Badge of Courage

If you have been unhappily stuck in a situation but lack the guts to make a change, it sounds as if you could use some courage. Courage is needed when fear is running some part of your life and it becomes your excuse for resisting change. There are so many kinds of excuses—"They won't let me change," "They might not accept me," "I'm too young, old, fat, stupid, boring"—so many I can't list them all. But all it takes is the courage to start. A little red goes a long way here. Just add anything red

You and your world are a product of your thoughts.

in the Fame and Reputation section to start the process. Even if you don't know where you are going, take action, and the next opportunity will show up.

Nine-to-Five Respect

Tammy finally got the accounting job she was looking for in a public institution. But when she got there, she noticed that some things weren't being handled very accurately or responsibly. She was determined to clean it up, but was met with resistance at every level, with top management actually saying to leave well enough alone. Tammy then found herself outside the organization's loop with social as well as professional matters. She called in a feng shui professional—my friend Nate.

He immediately started moving her office furniture around. "Facing the door when you sit at your desk is a must for anyone," he said as he placed her desk and chair in the Fame section of the office (see Figure 11). He suggested placing a wooden bookshelf on either side of her desk against the back wall (to "guard" her). Then he meticulously placed her accounting books on the shelves (to symbolically show everyone how meticulous she was). He told her to add silk plants on top of the shelves (to soften the shelves and subconsciously create trees out of them—"wood feeds fire"). Then, looking around the office for the perfect thing to hang on the wall behind her, he came upon some beautiful original art. "What's this?" he asked, sifting through the floral paintings.

"Oh, that's some art my grandmother did. She is a well-known artist in the country from which I came."

"Perfect. Place these behind you," he said. "They hold the

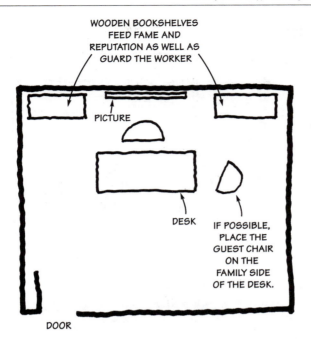

WOODEN BOOKSHELVES
FEED FAME AND
REPUTATION AS WELL AS
GUARD THE WORKER

PICTURE

DESK

IF POSSIBLE,
PLACE THE
GUEST CHAIR
ON THE
FAMILY SIDE
OF THE DESK.

DOOR

Desk should always face the office door but not line up with it.

FIGURE 11

energy of a respected person as well as having your grandmother watching out for you." (See Figure 12.) Tammy maintained her integrity and kept working.

It worked. After about two months, she said people were treating her with respect. After two years, she found an accounting error that everyone else had missed, and saved the institution millions and a bad reputation. Shortly after that, all the executives were asked to step down, and she was practically the last employee standing.

Your desk may be the only thing you are actually in charge of spatially at your office (see Figure 13). Make sure it gathers respect for you. If you have clientele, guests, or coworkers frequently meeting with you at your desk, have them sit on the Family side of the desk if at all possible. (Look back at

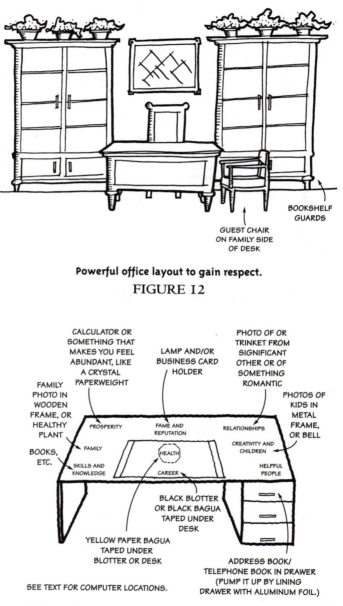

Powerful office layout to gain respect.

FIGURE 12

Feng shui your desk just like your home—the front door is where you sit.

FIGURE 13

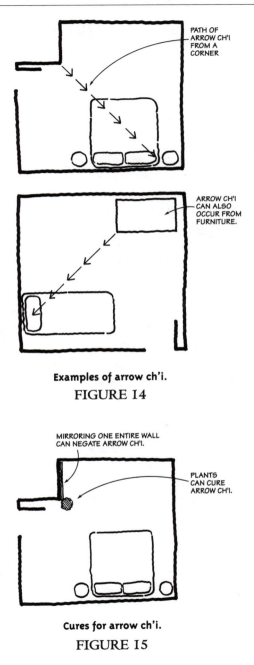

Examples of arrow ch'i.

FIGURE 14

Cures for arrow ch'i.

FIGURE 15

Figure 11). If you are the boss, come out from behind your desk to speak with others. If you aren't, and the boss comes to speak with you, be sure you are sitting at your desk.

Slings and Arrows

In feng shui the term *arrow ch'i* is used when a corner of the house, or of the room, or of a piece of furniture pokes into a living space (see Figure 14). It's kind of like that finger that always enters the picture to poke the Pillsbury Doughboy, but doesn't tickle quite as much. This type of energy causes great upheaval in the invisible land of ch'i, slinging all sorts of erratic energy out into the room. The whole home should be reviewed for this negative energy pattern, not just the Fame section. (Perhaps a quick reminder of this in your notebook is a good idea.) It's harsh on us humans, causing all sorts of weird ailments and behaviors, from physical aches and pains to habits like not wanting to sleep on a particular side of the bed or sit in a poorly situated chair.

If you have any of these arrows pointing in places where you spend most of your time—your bed, desk, or La-Z-Boy lounger in front of the tube—here are some feng shui choices:

1. Place a plant (hopefully one as tall as the ceiling) at the corner. (See Figure 15.)
2. Hang a crystal (one of those round glass multifaceted jobs) from the ceiling, out from the arrow corner a couple of inches. (See Figure 16.)
3. Mirror one whole side of the wall. This one can get costly and may not fit in with the decor. (See Figure 15.)
4. Move the bed, desk, or La-Z-Boy to another place, out of the line of fire.

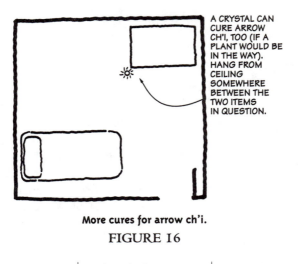

A CRYSTAL CAN CURE ARROW CH'I, TOO (IF A PLANT WOULD BE IN THE WAY). HANG FROM CEILING SOMEWHERE BETWEEN THE TWO ITEMS IN QUESTION.

More cures for arrow ch'i.
FIGURE 16

| Life of the Party |

The Fame and Reputation area of the home, room, or yard thrives on party energy—it stirs up and invigorates the ch'i, uplifting your reputation with your friends and acquaintances. Hugh Hefner and Wolfgang Puck built their reputations with parties. Get on the invite list of an exclusive bash and you know what it can do for your reputation. I'm still fondly remembered for the body-painting parties and the yearly exotic beer parties I threw in my twenties (I can't believe I'm putting this in a book). One thing for sure, most people think I'm fun—and to me, that's not such a bad thing to be known for.

Youth also helps with this good kind of ch'i. (See the Creativity and Children chapter for your personal party supplies!)

Life is a party where you bring your own (as in everything). Some people just aren't happy with what they brought.

| Fire and Ice |

The gua opposite Fame and Reputation in the bagua is Career (see Figure 17). Picture how these two are connected. If someone is talking trash about you all the time, it may be hard to keep your career afloat. These two work simultaneously to enhance the prospect of having a good reputation and a fulfilling career.

Add a little something extra to the Career gua with the intention of helping your reputation in the world. You may be surprised at the results. After doing this myself, I can't tell you how quickly I became known and recognized for my feng shui work. I used a strategically placed pair of black curtains to do the work for me. (You really have to have the right decor to pull off black curtains. So make sure you don't add anything that's too out of place. It may subconsciously aggravate you, thereby lowering your personal ch'i.)

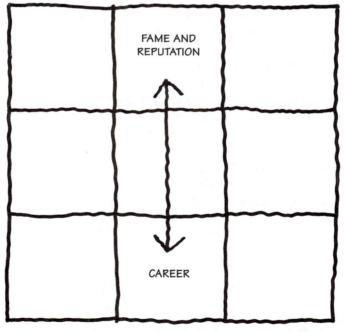

FIGURE 17

Eye'm Famous!

The eyes are the body part associated with the Fame and Reputation area of the home. If you are experiencing any trouble with your eyes, enhance this area with the intention of attracting positive ch'i for them.

One Is the Loneliest Number

The number associated with Fame and Reputation is the big numero uno. That's right: 1. After all, with fame or reputation, it's all about you and you alone. If you live in a 1 house (remember, add up all the numbers in the address as described in the last chapter), chances are you are being pulled to start new endeavors, like a business, a family, or a hobby. But, just as 1 is the first number, you might tend to think of yourself first and forget others. Sometimes this is good and sometimes it isn't—just a warning.

The best house for balancing a famous person is probably a 4 house. Although the Chinese have a thing against the number 4 (because the word for *die/death* and *four* are the same word in one of their dialects), a 4 home can be good for someone who is looking for stability and security. And with the lack of stability that sometimes comes with building your reputation, you might need a rock-solid foundation. Elvis Presley, Karen Carpenter, River Phoenix, Kurt Cobain, and John Belushi are a few good examples of people who became out of balance with fame. Insecurity can make people overcompensate in deadly ways.

Immediate Action Items for Fame and Reputation

1. Move any water that is movable out of the Fame section.
2. Add enhancements as necessary.

| Fame and Reputation in Summary |

Power Tools: fire, lights, red, triangular shapes, wood, green, television, rectangular or columnar shaped objects, items that represent fire, stained glass, animals and things made from animals, plants, pictures or memorabilia of celebrities or people you admire, recognition items, personal wish list, "up" stuff, real mountains.

Hazardous Materials: water, black, things that symbolize what you are *not* about, mirrors.

Opposite Gua: Career

Body Part: eye

Associated Number: I

chapter 4

Why Can't We All Just Get Along?—
Relationships and Love

f you lovingly move your stuff in the Relationship corner according to feng shui wisdom, you can enhance your life in many ways. You can

- ◉ find "the one"
- ◉ make a commitment without fear
- ◉ get married
- ◉ put the sizzle back into a relationship
- ◉ get along better with family, friends, and coworkers
- ◉ learn to trust people again.

Let's take the word *relationship*. The root word is *relate*. The question here is, how do things in your home relate to one another? How does your particular combination of household items affect how you relate to others on a subconscious level? Can you relate? Not yet? OK. Here's how it works. First you need to find the Relationship corner. It happens to be the back right-hand corner of the whole house, as you walk in the front door. (See Figure 18—and remember, Chapter 11 has solutions for missing pieces.) Enter here and hold on tight—you may not be alone tonight!

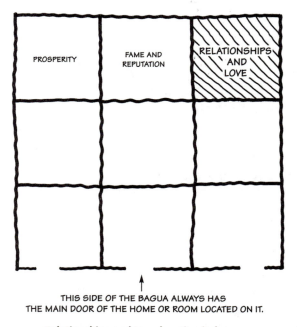

THIS SIDE OF THE BAGUA ALWAYS HAS
THE MAIN DOOR OF THE HOME OR ROOM LOCATED ON IT.

Relationships and Love location in bagua.

FIGURE 18

Just a Spent Fuel Rod in the Toxic Waste Dump of Love?

Are relationship blues causing you to consider a career as a sensory-deprivation-tank test volunteer? Whether you're looking for Mr./Mrs. Right or for Mr./Mrs. Right Now, here are some tips to help you in your search for a successful relationship.

Certain colors and objects reflect love. Pink, red, and white are excellent Relationship colors. Flowers and heart shapes are perfect Relationship objects. (See? Valentine's Day is not just a Hallmark holiday after all.) Just stick those things in your corner. It's that easy. It may sound crazy, but think of one thing about love that isn't.

Love is not a sight, a sound, or a taste (although in some cases it can be). It's a feeling, something emotional and intuitive.

It's intuition that makes feng shui work. So look around your home or room, and walk over to your Relationship corner. How does it feel? Loving? Probably not, or you'd be out on a date instead of reading this book. Focus your energy on this very special corner, carefully decorate it, and think loving thoughts. Then loving things will naturally happen in your life. I once knew a woman who, upon hearing about feng shui for the first time, walked over and threw a red pair of panties in her Relationship corner. She said to herself, "There, take that," and didn't give it another thought. A month later she was happily married to a millionaire. It could happen to you! But you have to want it and you have to do what it takes to make it happen. It all begins with awareness and action. Lights, camera, action— you are now the star of your own love story (and you get to decide what it's rated).

Be prepared for the avalanche of affection you discover on your new feng shui journey. At times it can seem like a landslide of love, a tsunami of sensuality, an earthquake of emotions. Bear in mind this caution: use the tools wisely and don't overdo it. Too many lovers and too much love can bring a whole new set of problems to your life. Then you'll need another book to solve those problems.

What is appropriate for your Relationship corner? Take a look.

Power Tools for Relationships and Love

Mirrors   Love is energy, and energy is a living thing. Control this energy by bouncing it around the room using mirrors. They work twenty-four hours a day, drawing in the light and energy so you can attract that special someone. Round ones work best here.

Candles   Candles generate heat and energy. Heat up your corner and heat up your love life. Try using one for each person in the relationship.

Hot Tub   It's about as hot and steamy as it gets.

Fresh Flowers   Dandelions from the crack in the sidewalk, or long-stem roses—if they're beautiful, fragrant, or full of life to you, they'll work here.

And continuing in the plant category: mistletoe is an obvious choice for love and relationships.

Think Pink   Soft, satiny, sensuous pink. Fresh, frosty, frilly pink. Pink feels like love, so let it color your corner. Add the Energizer bunny if you think there is a need to keep going and going . . .

Anything Red   The power is in the feeling of the color. Red hearts are obvious, but use what you have: a jar of maraschino cherries, a can of tomato soup (it worked for Andy Warhol), a silk scarf, a notebook, a red-hot chili pepper.

Undergarments   Does this really need an explanation?

Sensual Sounds   Since musical taste is in the ear of the beholder, you're on your own a little here. But I would venture to say, head-banging guitar or drum solos don't get Relationship ch'i in the mood.

Symbols That Mean Love to You   Come on. Get creative. You can do it. Here are some of my personal favorites:

- Barbie and Ken in formal bridal wear
- Barbie and G.I. Joe
- fireworks
- animal-print material
- a bottle of champagne and two glasses
- a bride-and-groom wedding cake decoration
- actually, two of just about anything—statues, lovebirds, plants, lights, pillows
- a bowl of passion fruit or Hershey's Kisses

(A man I knew had an old yellow ski lift sign above his bed that said *Singles Pair Up Here.* Tacky to me, but it worked for him.)

Equality   Make sure there is equality on both sides of the bed (whatever gua it falls into in the home). Two matching night-stands are best, even—*and especially*—if you are single. Don't take one of the matching tables and use it in another part of the house. This will cause imbalance in a relationship.

Hazardous Materials for Relationships and Love

Negative Images   Don't cloud your corner with unhappy thoughts. Pictures of ex-lovers, icebergs, limp noodles, riots, or the *Hindenburg* explosion won't foster loving thoughts. Thoughts are energy too, very much related to the energy of love.

"Unfriendly" Stuff   Cactus, Venus flytraps, and stinkweed plants do not a loving statement make. Lose the medieval weapon collection too.

"Frigid" Stuff   The air conditioner and refrigerator are work-ing against you if you want a hot love life.

"Single" Stuff   If you are stuck with a twin bed for now, at least invest in a guest pillow. Lose the photos of yourself alone in this corner. Take a look around and see if you have surrounded your-self with "single" symbols—especially art. I can't tell you how many feng shui consultations for relationship-seeking single women I have done where they have decorated their entire homes with art depicting women alone.

Games   You don't want to be playing games in your relation-ship, do you?

Uncleanliness   Creating a loving energy is difficult when dust balls, fingernail clippings, and old Twinkie wrappers clutter your corner.

Storage   That space under the bed looks like the perfect place to tuck away holiday wrapping paper, skis, and suitcases, but if you are looking for a relationship without a lot of baggage, clean it out. Having the area under your bed stuffed with stuff is the monster that makes us have bad dreams as adults.

Distractions   If your television is in the Relationship corner (especially if it also happens to be your bedroom), it may be getting in between you and your mate. If your computer is there, you may be more interested in surfing the Net than boogie-boarding with a loved one. If your ex-boyfriend's guitar is there, you may find yourself hanging on to that old song, rather than finding a new one.

If these things must stay, however, drape them, when not in use, with a nice fabric befitting the Relationship corner. The color cobalt blue is said to have EMF-negating properties, which may be a good idea for all those computer cords and screens.

Be open to change. The type of mate you desire may not be the best person for you. Forget old ideas of love. They didn't work before, so why carry those into the future? Keep your eyes peeled for new and improved expressions of love. They may come from where you least expect them.

Be Careful What You Wish For . . .

I know of someone who couldn't figure out what was wrong with her love life. All the men she attracted were married. Granted, they'd have been about perfect if they hadn't been married, but she didn't want to be the one to break up a marriage. She told me she had taken my advice, but it wasn't working. Months earlier, I had told her to write down what she was looking for in a man and place the paper in her Relationship corner. I asked her to show me the writing and had to laugh when I read the *banner* she had made for the corner: *I want a husband!* Well, that was exactly what she kept getting—husbands!

Be careful what you wish for because it may come back exactly how you ordered it. If you didn't get what you wanted, look again to see if it was what you asked for. It could have been all in the wording of your request. "Those" filling orders read them quite literally.

Really, My Seventeen Cats and I Are Fine, We Don't Need Anyone Else

If you are stuck in thinking that people are unnecessary in your life and that you have all you need right at home by yourself, you may want to rethink things a bit. Living the life of a hermit may be good if your intention is to watch your body hair grow. But if it comes from fear, mistrust, or anger, then you must start on the path to having relationships with people. Living alone didn't do much for Ted Kaczynski and it won't do much for you. Let's start by allowing people to feel comfortable coming to you. Walk out of your room or home and take a look with a visitor's eye at what you have to do to get inside. Is it unclear how to find your door? Is the path filled with clutter and other obstacles that hamper visitors? Is the address missing or confusing? Make sure there is a welcoming and orderly route to find you. Shine the door knocker, paint the door, place a pot with a flowering plant outside, open the shades, make your place inviting.

Then place photos of happy people in your Relationship corner. Better still, all around you. The more the better. If you don't have any, cut them out of magazines, get them off the Internet, or clip the Snap, Crackle, and Pop characters off the cereal box. Just surround yourself with people! You can also use any of the traditional ancient Chinese cures from Chapter I, like hanging a chime or a crystal in the corner, or placing a new healthy plant there. Get used to it, and then go out and get into the real world. Perhaps by placing your telephone in that corner you will be inclined to make calls that generate relationships (discontinue if it only gets you long-distance relationships). Tie

It's always a good idea to enhance your Family gua along with your Relationship gua. This will help connect you with people who will treat you like part of their family. Whether in business or amid marital bliss, it usually helps to be bonded in this way. (See Chapter 9.)

a red ribbon on the incoming cord to invigorate the ch'i and stimulate more calls.

People. People who need people . . . listen to Babs on this one.

Back Off and Nobody Gets Hurt

If life is miserable because there is a certain person who won't leave you alone, try this: place a cactus in your Fame section (I repeat: *Fame* section) with the exact intention of keeping this *specific* person away from you. Although it is a feng shui nightmare to have a cactus in the Relationship corner, it can be used in Fame. The Fame and Relationship areas work well together because the Fame area helps garner respect for you. If you use the cactus there, you will be respected and left alone. If it is a person you work with, try placing a small cactus in the Fame area of your desk (see Figure 13 in Chapter 3 for desk bagua layout) with the intention that the coworker leave you alone. If you are unsure of how to *intend* this to be so, simply place the cactus in the location and say either out loud or to yourself, "Matilda (or whoever), leave me alone." Then you can pump up the feng shui with some of the tips outlined in Chapter 12. Remember—cactus plants are allowed in the Fame and not the Relationship gua.

Mirrors are another way of ricocheting those goobers out of your life. But you have to be careful. You may stir up solutions that you didn't have in mind. I know of a woman who had been divorced for over a year and still shared the same house *and bed* with her husband. She wanted him to leave, so she placed a mirror against the wall directly at his head as he lay in bed. This disrupted him so much that he rooted around, found the mirror, and removed it. She placed another mirror there, and out of nowhere he started sleeping with his feet at the head of the bed. Last I heard, she happily said, "Problem solved. I bought my own house and moved out." I'll leave it up to you to figure out if this cure worked or not.

My Roommates Are Driving Me Crazy

Now let's talk about problem relationships with people other than lovers. They could be siblings, parents, friends, coworkers, the bitchy checkout girl at the mall—anyone in your life whose vibes are clashing with yours.

First try a simple solution. Write their name on a piece of paper along with yours. Remember the colors? Try red or pink. Perhaps cut it into a heart shape. Place it in the corner. Maybe you have a whole slew of people you need to have better relations with. Place each of them on a separate paper (unless they somehow go together).

I consulted on a new hair salon where there were six equal partners. Although everyone seemed excited about their venture, they were concerned that they might not always see eye-to-eye with business decisions and would need relationship help in the future. We immediately addressed the situation. They wrote all their names on the drywall and drew one big heart around them all before the wall was painted. They know that heart will be under that paint forever. It has been one year since the salon opened, and no squabbles yet! Once again, you don't even have to see the feng shui to have it work for you.

Not Always the Bridesmaid

Perhaps the question I most often get asked in my practice is, "How do I find *the one*?" Here's the answer: start with a thorough cleaning of the Relationship area. If you want to clean the entire room or rooms that fall into this area, so much the better.

Do this to clear out all of the past relationships that didn't work.

Sometimes you can instinctively use feng shui without even knowing it. My friend Melody threw out every item in her house that was pink, including her phone, dishes, and all articles of clothing with pink in them. This was before she knew anything about feng shui. I explained what she was doing from a feng shui point of view, and she said that indeed she wanted to stop attracting the same wrong men. It was truly symbolizing "Out with the old, in with the new" in regard to her relationships.

Another thing to do is look at the bed and its location in the bedroom. Even if it is not a part of the Relationship gua in the home, it strongly affects Relationship ch'i. Just as the stove is a symbol of Prosperity wherever it is in the home, the bed symbolizes Relationships anywhere.

What do your bed and bedroom say about you? Are they inviting? Does it feel like there is room enough for another person in the room or the bed? If one side of the bed is jammed up against the wall, pull it out and perhaps set up a little nightstand for the future lover. Decorate it with things you hope will appeal to them.

The best way to achieve optimum results when you are building your Relationship area is to be in the frame of mind that you are doing this solely for the creation of a loving relationship with someone who is perfect for you. It may be a leap of faith for some, but asking for "the perfect person for me" rather than for a specific person by name will result in the best mate in the world, rather than the best mate among the people you know now. Odds are better with the first way. Trust me.

Sleeping Single in a Double Bed

As I stated above, surrounding yourself with "single" stuff does not lead to a life overwhelmed with love interests. Pay special attention to the Relationship corner of your bedroom and be sure you are not giving off "I Prefer to Sleep Alone" signals if that is not your preference.

There was a woman who wanted love but had a huge painting of a woman alone staring down at her from this bedroom corner. When the symbolism of being alone was explained, she replied, "That's interesting. I'm a twin and I have always been searching for a singular identity. Since I put that picture there, I have been more autonomous with her than ever before." Unfortunately, she became autonomous with everyone else, too. (A better cure would be to use another item with specific intention to gain autonomy only from the twin.)

My So-Called Wife

Sara and Marty fell madly in love and got married. Everything was perfect. They decided to get a dog, thinking it would be good training for the future responsibility of having children. They got a beautiful golden retriever, along with all the fixin's— the toys, the brushes, the food, and a beautiful bed. They came home and placed the dog's bed in the corner of their bedroom so they could all sleep safely together. Unfortunately, the Relationship corner was where the dog's bed landed. Suddenly, everything was about the dog. It didn't take long for it to start coming between them—literally, in their bed. They thought it was cute at first—he was so small and cuddly. But then they noticed they didn't have the time or energy to even think of raising kids, what with all this dog stuff. After all, he was going to school now! I asked Marty one day about having children and he said he and Sara were working on their relationship first. I was shocked. I had to take a look around. Upon inspecting the Relationship corner, I quickly told him about how important this corner was to their relationship and that they had created a threesome with the dog. He said it felt that way, and now he had a new determination to get his wife back. The dog's bed moved,

> Whatever resides in the Relationship corner besides you and your partner may falsely seem more important than your relationship. At a minimum, it may wiggle its way between the two of you, looking for equal attention.

and so did the energy. They are happily working on having those kids they said they always wanted.

Yo Quiero "Cu-ch'i Cu-ch'i"

Perhaps you are in a relationship but are looking to spice up your sex life. Maybe you are single and want to get a little more than you have been lately. Whatever the circumstance, let's talk about sex—steamy, sticky, sultry sex. Now, I am separating sex from quality, loving relationships here to better illustrate how to get exactly what you want. If sex is your goal, place symbols of physical pleasure such as massage books, oils, condoms, smutty magazines, sex toys, trashy lingerie, and aphrodisiacs in your Relationship area. How about burning one of those sex-chakra candles?

If your mate isn't as frisky as you would like him or her to be, place red under the bed, perhaps a red scarf or cloth under the mattress. Red is an energy activator. I know of a woman who placed the red under her husband's side only because she thought he needed to catch up with her sexual appetite. To her amazement, after about one month she found herself removing it because he was now more frisky than she!

You don't have any of these things lying around to create your sex den? Shame on you! Well, then cut them out of magazines and make a montage in the area. Or place the pictures in a secret box in the space. Now, since this is merely a physical thing you are looking for, I would spice up the Health area as well. Go to the center of the home or room and place something that appeals to both your physical health and pleasure, such as facial mud (remember, the element in this area is earth). Or maybe burn some long, hot, dripping flesh-toned candles (fire makes earth). Are you starting to see the possibilities?

And finally, since you need help from another person to achieve your goal of sex, you may want to spice up your Helpful People area. You can be as extravagant as you want. A simple solution is to write, "I have awesome sex easily available to me," on a paper placed in the area. The bagua color for the Helpful People area is silver or gray, so place the paper in a silver box if you have one. An extravagant way is having a chrome or silver sculpture of fornicating couples in the area. A cheap way is to use aluminum foil around the paper request. Go with what appeals to your lifestyle and budget.

Try to appease each of the senses when you are creating your love den. Here are some quick ideas:

- *smell*—scented candles or lotions, fresh flowers (no deodorizers from a can)
- *touch*—velvet, silk, tassels, leather, feathers (no rough, dry hands allowed)
  sound—music, ocean waves, thunderstorm, crackling fire (no sports on TV)
- *sight*—soft lighting, sexy undergarments (no piles of laundry or pictures of Mom)
- *taste*—chocolate, whipped cream, champagne, strawberries (vacuum yesterday's cookie crumbs off the bed, please)

Our karmic makeup is designed so that we come to this earth to serve and love ourselves as well as others. Please be clear that if you choose sex for sex's sake, choose it for the sheer joy of the physical pleasure or your ability to please another physically, not because of power, control, dominance, or self-confidence issues. These conditions may cause you to create additional karma to be resolved at another time.

The Revolving Door to My Bedroom

Where you sleep has a lot of impact on your personal energy. It can affect your health, mental attitude, and love life as much as anything. Remember, even if the bedroom is not in the Relationship gua, it still may affect relationships. Things to look for around your bed:

Doors If a door is in a direct line with your bed (see Figure 19) you may be experiencing health problems in the area of your body that is closest to the door. If it is at the foot of your bed, your feet may stink or you may have weak ankles or shin splints. If the door hits the middle of the bed on one side, perhaps you may be experiencing problems with organs on that side (as you lie on your back in bed), or the person that sleeps on that side may have health problems there. Move your bed out of this alignment. If there is no alternative location and the door is at the foot of the bed, try placing a trunk at the foot of the bed and placing a mirror of some kind inside it facing toward the door to reflect it away from the bed. Another alternative would be to place red items in the trunk to slow the flow. No trunk?

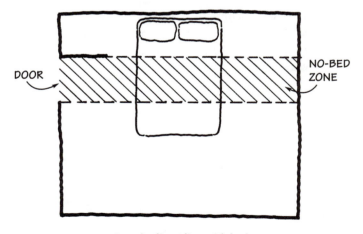

Door in direct line with bed.
FIGURE 19

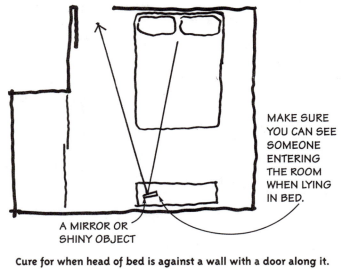

MAKE SURE YOU CAN SEE SOMEONE ENTERING THE ROOM WHEN LYING IN BED.

A MIRROR OR SHINY OBJECT

Cure for when head of bed is against a wall with a door along it.

FIGURE 20

How about a red bench or chair? No furniture? Tape a red ribbon across the bottom of the bed frame.

Also, try not to place the head of your bed against the wall that has the door along it—you don't want someone startling you as you sleep. If this is the only location you have, place a shiny object or mirror in a location that reflects the door to you while in bed (see Figure 20).

Windows Do not place the head of your bed under a window. Who needs Romeo scaring the PJs off you in the middle of the night when he comes a-tapping? If there is no alternative, place a red item (or a symbol—like a little toy Doberman pinscher) on the sill to protect you. Wooden shutters may also be helpful.

Beams Wherever a visible beam cuts across your bed, it severs that part of your body. I'm talking about structural beams here, not light or laser beams. Serious health issues can arise. If it runs between you and your partner's side of the bed, you will have to expend most of your energy overcoming that beam, which is dividing you from your partner (see Figure 21). If beams are

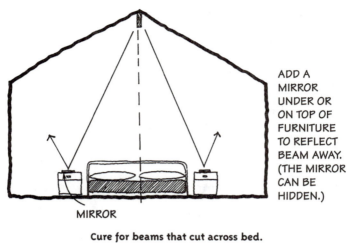

ADD A MIRROR UNDER OR ON TOP OF FURNITURE TO REFLECT BEAM AWAY. (THE MIRROR CAN BE HIDDEN.)

MIRROR

Cure for beams that cut across bed.
FIGURE 21

inevitable, place a mirror on your nightstands facing up to lighten the load of the beams over you. Another, more decorative cure would be to take a piece of fabric at least as big as the bed and tack it to the ceiling directly over the bed in a billowy, upholstered look (maybe with ornaments or tassels at tack points). Then, when you look up while lying in your bed, you will see a romantic, luxurious fabric not unlike a canopy bed cover, rather than the arrow-slinging beams (see Figure 22).

CREATE A SOFT CANOPY OVER THE BED WITH A NICE PIECE OF FABRIC WHEN BEAMS ARE OVERHEAD.

Another cure for beams that cut across bed.
FIGURE 22

One final cure is to draw arrows on the sides of the beams, pointing up. Weird, huh? "Beam me up, Scotty!"

Ceilings   Try not to locate your bed under a sloping ceiling. Wherever the ceiling lowers, your energy gets smashed (see Figure 23). For example, if the ceiling slopes down toward the head of your bed, you may experience such ailments as headaches, forgetfulness, and sinus conditions. Again, place mirrors facing up somewhere in this location (under or on a night stand, and so forth) if it is your only option for bed placement.

Protruding Corners (Creating Arrow Ch'i)   If your bedroom has a corner protruding into it, try to avoid having it point at your bed. Use one of the cures stated in the last chapter, like placing a plant at the corner; or try to visually erase it by hanging a mobile or crystal in front of the corner.

Mirrors   If you sit up in your bed and see your reflection in a mirror in front of you, try to block it out. Those full-length sliding mirrored closet doors can give you the willies at night.

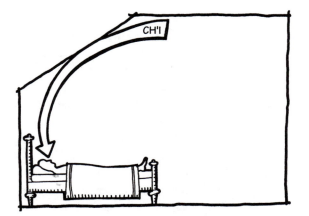

The part of the bed (head, side, or foot) that is under a sloped ceiling is the part of the body that gets squished by negative ch'i.

FIGURE 23

Hang curtains that can be pulled across the doors at night, or try using a folding screen.

If you have mirrors on the ceiling, get out of the seventies.

Elements   What's the bed made of? Perhaps the main element making the bed is playing against your favor. So, let's play the element "rock, paper, scissors" game.

A wooden bed is OK just about everywhere except in the middle of the room, where the wood would uproot the earth section. (Add yellow and green if that is your only option.) Do not put a metal bed in the Family section of the room, as metal cuts wood. It is best in the Creativity section. Get that water bed out of the Fame section. It's best in the Family section, where water feeds wood.

Remember, the bagua of a room is found just as the bagua of the entire house is—by aligning the Skills and Knowledge, Career, and Helpful People guas up with the wall that the door is on.

What Good Could Come of This?

I had a client, Meranda, who called me to feng shui her home before her husband, Rob, returned from the hospital. The doctors were treating him for a broken hip and intestinal problems (yes, he had the bathroom door ch'i plowing into him in his hip area of the bed). While in the hospital, Rob started becoming delusional and paranoid. Eventually, they wanted to keep him, not because of his original problems but because of his new mental condition.

I worked on the home with all my might, and miraculously, Rob turned a corner and was released. Rob made recovery headway that astounded the doctors. They told him to keep up whatever he was doing.

Almost fully recovered, he decided to run an errand. While driving, he was involved in what was, at first, an extremely minor fender bender, in which his head jerked and tapped the window.

From all accounts, the accident looked like no big deal, but it put Rob into a health-compromising tailspin in which his seemingly minor maladies quickly took his life. (In hindsight, Meranda thinks that Rob was supposed to pass in the hospital, and due to the feng shui, she got some extra time with him.)

But that's not where the story ends. During the year after Rob died, Meranda slowly cleared out Rob's things and started making small changes to the home. After about one year, she decided to rearrange the bedroom and buy a new mattress. While moving the armoire, she found Rob's wallet—one of his last personal effects still at home. She had misplaced it a year earlier. But now, she was finally able to let it go. Symbolically and energetically, she closed one door, which allowed another to open. With the exception of a few pieces of furniture, the bedroom (and the ch'i) was now totally different than when Rob was alive.

Then Meranda, who was Catholic by upbringing (Rob was Jewish), decided to look into converting to Judaism. She and Rob had discussed converting when he was alive, but he thought it was not necessary. One day, while in temple, she started conversing with a gentleman from London who was in town visiting a friend. They quickly found out they were in the same boat with regard to having lost their spouses. The British gentleman asked if he could see her again before he left town.

"The only reason I agreed was because I knew he was flying back to London soon. It was safe. I had not a thought of dating in my mind," Meranda confessed. They became almost inseparable during his remaining time in the States and have been in contact over the phone quite often ever since.

Although his entire family and his successful business are in London, he recently purchased a condo near her home in the States. "We've decided to just see what happens," Meranda said. She ended our conversation with, "I'm happier than I ever thought I could be."

The morals of the story are:

1. When it's your time to go, it's your time (give or take a little with feng shui, perhaps).

2. Be on the lookout for opportunities. If the British gent hadn't been British (just a visitor), Meranda said, she would have turned him down, cutting herself off from the universal flow. She would have passed up her chance for happiness without even knowing it.

3. If you think feng shui has stopped working for you because something dreadful has happened, think again. Even though you cannot possibly see anything good from such a tragic event, trust that the universe can.

Love is an energy. Energy is a living thing. Therefore, to live fully we all need to give love and receive love. And if you have taken the time to feng shui your Relationship corner, it is no longer just a corner. It is a shrine to *amour.* Now every time you look over there, you'll think loving thoughts. And since thoughts are also energy and very much related to the energy of love, when you think loving thoughts, loving things will naturally begin to happen in your life.

"Come In—May I Take Your Clothes?"

While we're on the subject of beds, when you walk in the front door, make sure that you do not see the bed first. If you are in a studio apartment or dorm room, place an object that catches your eye upon entering, to distract the first look from your bed. Try placing a folding screen between the bed and the rest of the apartment during the day, or make it look like a couch, with accessories like pillows and end tables. If you have to pass through your bedroom to get to other parts of the house, like the bathroom, apply the same cure to take your eye to another object rather than the bed. From a great piece of art to a glittery jar full of colorful hair scrunchies, use your imagination to make it work for you. Blocking the bed from first view not only helps avoid inviting too much sexual energy into one's life; it also helps if you sleep too much—so, sleepaholics take note as well.

| I'll Never Trust Again |

If the ashes are still smoldering from your last relationship and you feel you would rather walk into a lava pit than get into a new one, listen up. It just sounds like that ol' trust button is stuck and needs a little lube job. Trusting another with your heart is risky business. It's like a roller-coaster ride without a safety belt—at a minimum, you'll have bruises. But love *is* about trusting, and without love and trust, the ride of life somehow seems meaningless. Oh sure, you could be telling yourself, "Hey, who needs to be kicked around? Not me. I'll be fine reading feng shui books and doing crossword puzzles the rest of my life."

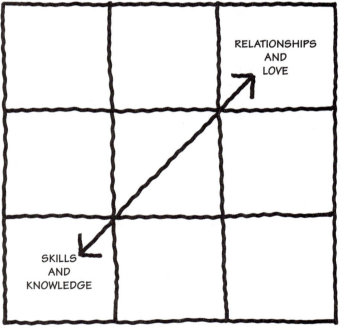

FIGURE 24

If you go around looking for the worst in everyone, *trust me,* you'll find it. It's amazing how powerful your attitude and perception are when dealing with your life experiences. Take me for example. I call myself a "Hyatt camper." My idea of roughing it is *no room service.* But other people simply love to sleep in their clothes on the ground, dig a hole for a toilet, and wash their dishes in a stream. Different perceptions at work. So, where do we go from here?

Let's work on the perception. Get your Relationship corner in order—a junky one attracts junky relationships. Start off by making a place to nurture yourself. Often, when you don't trust others, you actually don't trust yourself. Allow yourself time to grow into the feeling of trusting your decisions. Perhaps an affirmation about trust is in order. Change that broken record in your mind that says something like "Nobody really cares about me" to "I experience love wherever I am."

Make sure the Skills and Knowledge corner is addressed. It's the opposite gua from Relationships and Love (see Figure 24). Place a reminder of trust in this area as well, to counterbalance the energy throughout. Perhaps write an affirmation like "I trust myself and the universe to make the best decisions for my highest good" or "I no longer need and now release the experience that has created lack of trust," and place it in the corner.

Now, let's go to the Fame and Reputation wall and do a little something extra there. This area of the bagua is associated with courage, which may be just the thing needed to get started on this process. A pink candle is the easy answer for this cure, since fire is the element for this gua and pink is the color for the Relationship gua next to it. Get one of those seven-day candles to light if you need a jump start.

The Organ Trail

Follow the trail of logic with this one: The relationship area is associated with all organs of the body. Heart/relationship, get it? So, if there's a problem with the ol' ticker or any other non-musical organ, enhance this area to make it better. (Of course, continue seeing your doctors.)

It Takes Two to Tango

The number 2 holds the essence for relationships, for obvious reasons. If you live in a 2 house, you probably find yourself quite in sync with your mate, spouse, or partner. You'll also have little need to depend on outsiders for anything (which can be good or bad, depending on how you look at it).

The challenging address to live at for relationships is—as you've probably guessed—number 1. Be vigilant with your enhancements if you want a relationship and live in a 1 home.

Immediate Action Items for Relationships and Love

1. Remove withering or dead stuff.
2. Review your bed and bedroom for arrow ch'i and other feng shui faux pas.
3. Add enhancements as necessary.

Relationships and Love in Summary

Power Tools: mirrors, candles, hot tub, fresh flowers, pink, red, undergarments, sensual sounds, symbols that mean love to you, equality.

Hazardous Materials: negative images, "unfriendly" stuff, "frigid" stuff, "single" stuff, games, uncleanliness, storage, distractions.

Opposite Gua: Skills and Knowledge

Body Part: all major organs of the body

Associated Number: 2

chapter 5

Express Yourself—
Creativity and Children

 eing imaginative with your stuff in the Creativity and Children area of the home can result in life changes. You can

- become able to conceive and bear children
- find fulfillment and gratification with a hobby or job have better, more creative ideas for every situation
- get unstuck in a project
- improve your relationship with your children
- become more comfortable showing the childlike side of your personality
- make "something out of nothing"
- create efficiency in a company
- deter the aging process

It's time to get creative. Are you ready? This chapter can be a lot of fun because the more imaginative you get with your cures, the more activated the gua gets, which in turn allows you to be more creative, and so on and so on.

Why are Children and Creativity lumped into one area of the house? you ask. The reason is that children are the embodi-

ment of creation. They are the epitome of creatively transform-
ing energy and intention into matter. But don't think that having kids is solely what this area of your home is about. This spot
in your home can help you with personal creativity in your work,
hobby, decision making, fashion, relaxation, and self-cultivation,
as well as in your relationships with your family, friends, and, of
course, lovers. And come on, who couldn't use a little creativity
in their love life?

Children think freely—as if anything is possible. They know
no limitations. Those darling rug rats continually ask adults,
"Why?" because they naturally and instinctively think, "Why
not?" They have not yet been programmed to define themselves
negatively like most adults. They express their thoughts, no matter how un-PC, to anyone they choose. They aren't afraid to
draw a tree with blue leaves or a horse with a pink head—until
some adult chimes in to squish their creative freedom.

If this area is enhanced correctly, you may be able to regain
your childlike creativity again. From your front door, skip over to
the area located in the middle of the right-hand wall of your home
(see Figure 25). Now you are smack dab in the middle of the Creativity center of your home. Look at it with your new feng shui
eyes. What is it saying about you? If you saw this stuff in someone
else's home, would you think they are free to express themselves or
be creative? If not, here is the stuff you can use to make it that way.

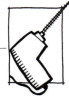

Power Tools for Creativity and Children

Metal   Metal is the element for this area of the home—so, the
more metal, the merrier. Some friends of mine who placed a
silver baby rattle in this area found the process of their two
adoptions unusually easy. A landscape architect friend had a
blacksmith create two iron sconces of calla lilies for his Creativity wall. If this area falls in the kitchen, you can make your pots
and pans help you become more creative with your cooking.
Some of the best items I have found to announce the new cre-

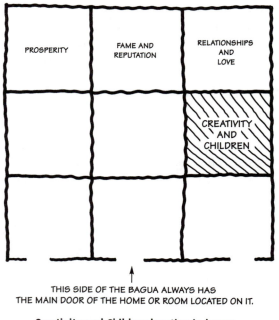

THIS SIDE OF THE BAGUA ALWAYS HAS
THE MAIN DOOR OF THE HOME OR ROOM LOCATED ON IT.

Creativity and Children location in bagua.

FIGURE 25

ativity in a home are musical instruments, metal bells, and wind chimes. Make sure the sounds are pleasant to you.

Living in a motel or dorm room and don't have that kind of stuff? Place your loose coins, eating utensils, metal picture frames, or jewelry box here. Remember to think of the objects in a literal way when choosing them: a metal toolbox may lead you to become known for your talents as a creative handyman. If you don't mind that, fine. If you do, find another chunk of metal (brass, bronze, copper, gold, iron, silver, and stainless steel are just a few).

White   The color for Creativity is white. Look around and see what's white that can activate your creative side. Got milk? If your kitchen is in this area, you can use your carton of milk to get you thinking more creatively as kids do. Drink milk out of a bowl. Drink it and laugh real hard until it comes out of your nose. And don't forget the graham crackers and Oreos.

I know someone who bought a white car for her Creativity zone garage—what a big hunk of white metal that is!

Think of an art gallery with white walls—it is ready to accommodate an unlimited number of styles and materials. Is your space free to flow with your unlimited creative possibilities, like a gallery? Now think of a dark-paneled room with a chocolate brown shag carpet and a ceiling so low you can reach up and touch it flatfooted. The only creative thoughts coming out of people in a room like this are quick exit plans. Find a balance for Creativity in your home.

Round Stuff   The shape for metal in feng shui is round, or circular. Time to get a round metal clock for the wall, perhaps? If not, scan your place for round stuff and put it here—round pillows for the couch, round cans in the cabinet. I have a white round metal floor lamp in my Creativity area. Sure, that Frisbee collection works. So does that plate collection. An outdoor-type friend of mine hangs his expensive bike inside here. (Did the Chinese think about round metal bicycle spokes and wheels when they figured this stuff out?)

Earth   Remember, earth creates metal in the Creative Cycle. So get creative with earth. A plant in a round ceramic pot filled with earth is a great ch'i enhancer for this area. A client of mine had one of those tiny globe key chains lying around doing nothing. She set it on her metal bookshelf to see what would happen. Within six months she was given a new position at work that required world travel—a secret dream of hers. She now says it was her key chain that unlocked her dream of seeing the world. (You will find in the next chapter that the gua adjacent to this one includes Travel. It appears that she raised the ch'i so much that it spilled into the adjacent areas of the home.)

Yellow   Since the color yellow represents earth, it is appropriate to place it here. Those round ceramic pots above would be even better if they were painted white or yellow. A client who wanted a baby placed three plants in small yellow pots (signifying her husband, herself, and a child) in her Children area. With

The power of intention really has no boundaries or limits except the ones we place on it.

your imagination, intention, and stuff like yellow curtains, towels, or dishes you can help create your dream life.

Flat or Square Stuff   These shapes mean earth in feng shui terms. Placing them here, you are adding earth to the space. If you have a wrought iron coffee table nearby, intend it to work for your creativity. If you're into computers, store your three-and-a-half-inch discs and CDs in this area. Square metal frames are picture perfect hung on these walls. My brother has a marble chess set that works for him—a game for children and adults alike—full of squares and made from one of the earth's more beautiful materials.

Television   This is the best place to watch Saturday-morning cartoons.

Toys and Games   And with the TV comes Nintendo and Play-Station. Any and all games—especially your favorites—can help activate this area of the home. The only caveat to this one: if your Creativity space falls in the master bedroom, just make sure things don't get too juvenile in there and that there is no game playing in your relationship.

Candy   Tasty reminders of the joy of childhood can spark the kid in all of us. From saltwater taffy and candy buttons to Skittles and Nerds, pick the sugar buzz that gives you the best memories. This is a great spot for that PEZ dispenser or bubble gum card collection.

Magic Tricks   These games are especially good because they take a lot of imagination to create and perform. If you are into magic, place your hat and wand here.

Parties   Like Fame, this spot loves the energy of a party. So go ahead, throw that body-painting party you've been dreaming about since I mentioned it earlier. (Tip: use water-based paint!)

Music   Crank up the stereo and fill your space with musical creations. This spot will gladly accept any musical style from soft sounds to hard rock. Receivers, speakers, and music collections all help the creative energy in this location.

Art   This consummate symbol of creativity performs like no other in this area. Pick something you love to be your symbol of imagination.

Hobbies or Crafts   Unless it is juggling flaming torches (you don't want fire melting your metal), you may be the most creative with your hobbies and crafts here.

Bed   Looking for some new, creative positions? Then move your bed into the Creativity position of the room.

Lightbulbs or Lights   Having bright ideas is what this symbolizes. Just make sure they are plugged in and in working order. They don't even have to be on to help you be creative.

Bells   A metal bell is a fantastic way to enhance your creativity. Given the right intention, a bell can do many things. It can stimulate creativity, focus attention, become a warning device, interrupt negativity, or even say thank you.

> Bells don't have to be ringing, chimes don't have to be moving, and crystals don't have to be reflecting light to be working for you in feng shui.

If you place a small bell in the Creativity area of your desk (see Figure 13, Chapter 3, for desk layout), it will stimulate creativity in business, Skills and Knowledge, and focus your attention to the task at hand. If it is protection you are looking for, place a small bell on or in whatever you are looking to protect—your purse, briefcase, laptop, car, or the front door to your home. This tiny, innocent little sound can be very unnerving to people with thievery on their mind.

Ring a bell in the company of people who need to come to a decision. It will cut down the time dramatically. My friend Susan was asked to work with a particular designer who took too long to make decisions. They were working on a big, high-profile event. His indecisiveness was affecting her work and pushing the deadlines. She pinned a small bell to her jacket, and whenever she needed a decision from him, she rang the bell. As if trained by Pavlov himself, he responded to her questions quickly and, to his own amazement, quite creatively. The conversations they had were "clear as a bell." Susan swears the project would have never been pulled off without the bell.

Just as the teachers of old used to ring a bell to gather the children together or make them pay attention, ring a bell to get coworkers or friends to stop gossiping or having backbiting conversations. Try it. Watch them stop, look at the bell, and discontinue their negative train of thought. Sure, they may think you're loony, but who cares? It really works!

A bell can also be a great tool in business. Ring it to announce the closing of a deal or to announce a big sale. Remember the ringing of the old cash registers? The bells were ringing cash into the register and saying a kind thank-you back to the customer—a much happier experience than today's beeping scanners and humming computers.

Matthew bought a failing hair salon. At his new salon, the manicurists were always in mini catfights, slinging nasty names at one another like kids on a playground. The stylists were unenthusiastic, which made for very few appointments. He knew the salon needed help when he bought it. He also knew he could trust feng shui to turn it around.

Upon the advice of his feng shui consultant, he got a bell. He gave it to the receptionist and told her to ring it every time she booked an appointment. It started out slowly, but each time she rang the bell, the bitchy manicurists would stop their conversations midstream and usually didn't go back to them for a while. Eventually, everyone got excited when they heard the bell ring, wondering if the appointment was for them. In a short time, the bell was ringing a lot and the employees were positive and excited about working there. Soon, Matthew saw profits. The only thing that was changed in the equation between the successful and unsuccessful owners was the introduction of the bell.

Symbols of Creativity   A child's finger painting is one of my favorite items that expresses creativity. Take a moment to think of what statement you would like to make in your home. I have seen ch'i enhancers that included everything from Mozart to Madonna, from the Egyptian pyramids to I. M. Pei's glass pyramid at the Louvre. Find your favorite poetry or music and accommodate them here. It's all about what you think is the ultimate in creativity, so don't worry about anybody else's opinion.

Symbols of Children   If you are trying to bring children into your life through adoption or childbirth, enhance this area of the home with things that give the illusion that they are already here. A couple of well placed Teletubbies can do a lot more than you think. (If you don't know what Teletubbies are, you're really in for a treat when the kids do arrive.)

Hazardous Materials for Creativity and Children

Of course, if there is good stuff to put in this space, there must be some not-so-good stuff too. Here are some of the worst.

Fire   The stuff that melts metal is not welcome here. If you've got a fireplace in this area, you have compromised metal. The most often used cure for this condition is to place a mirror that visually dominates the fireplace. In feng shui terms, you are placing water over the fire. It is also helpful to have a metal grate in front of the fireplace, or perhaps have the mirror in a metal frame. A friend in Florida placed her aquarium inside the fireplace for a creative water cure since she used it so little. A row of small vases along the mantel—each holding water and a single flower—makes a dramatic and fun cure. Carved ducks and fish can allude to water as well. A painting with black or blue as the dominant color introduces cool water symbolically. Candles are not good mantel subjects in this sector.

A client of mine who spent tons of money and time trying to get pregnant had a historic photograph about three feet long hanging in her Children section. Unfortunately it was of the 1906 earthquake in San Francisco, complete with homes a-blazin'. In other words, no disasters, please.

Red Stuff   Red keeps this area heated up—not what metal likes. I have seen a red silk Japanese kimono hung over a fireplace here that eventually "burnt out" a couple from pursuing their dream of owning their own business.

Triangular or Pointy Objects   Since these shapes represent fire, it's best to leave them out of this space. Eat your bowl of Doritos somewhere else, my friend.

When the Feng Shui Wind Blows, the Cradle Will Rock

People's inability to successfully conceive and bear children has been such a significant portion of my practice that I am going to dwell on this topic a bit. Given the impatience of those who want a baby, here are a few generic feng shui tips to use for conception:

- ◉ Don't sweep under or around the bed. Because you want energy to settle in, don't stir it up by vacuuming. Gently and slowly clean the bedroom area as needed. Helpful hint—clip those toenails outside.
- ◉ Enhance the Children section of the home with things for a new baby. You must give each item the intention of being for "the baby that is already on its way." Strongly visualize using these items on the baby. If these items

only remind you of what you want but don't have, it will slow the process even more.

◉ Place a spiritual or religious object in the bedroom that can be seen from bed. Do this with the intention of surrendering yourself to a higher power (for example, Mother and Child).

◉ Affirm your desire. If you are buying into your negativity and perhaps the negativity of others and feel totally hopeless about ever getting pregnant, say something like, "My seemingly impossible wish now comes to pass, and the unexpected now happens. Thank you for the gift of creating the new life within." Say it over and over until you believe it. Release all incompatible thoughts.

I have heard of people rubbing a fertility statue and swearing it works, and I have heard of people spending $40,000 on fertility stuff and getting nowhere. Take an inner inventory of what your mind chatters about in regard to this matter. If it is saying, "This is hopeless, I'll never get pregnant," you will have an uphill battle to fight. Fight back with affirmations.

◉ Don't hammer nails into your house or do any major renovations while trying to conceive. Once again, this stirs up the energy as well as temporarily unsettling the house.

◉ Partly fill a bowl with clean water. Take it outside at night and place it in the moonlight for at least three hours. Bring it in and place it under the bed in the vicinity of the woman's abdomen. Do this for nine days. Pump up the feng shui with the visualizations and blessings discussed in Chapter 12. (Considered a traditional cure, this ritual relies on extended intention and the moon's yin energy to work.)

Banishing the Balancing Bunnies

My friend consulted with a client who moved into a home that had the Creativity and Children corner of her home missing. She had a miscarriage after moving in and was also considering changing careers because she just wasn't inspired any longer— she was a children's clothing designer. It's hard to get creative about designing children's clothing with your Children and Creativity section of the home missing!

When the consultant went outside to see what was actually in the missing piece, the owner said, "When I first moved in here, two rabbits decided to make this area their home and actually had babies here. But they started to eat the plants, so I called someone and had them removed." From a feng shui standpoint the rabbits were exactly what she needed—moving, living, *breeding* objects. But she took it all away. The rabbits were actually balancing the home but she didn't know any better and reversed her own fate.

They went back inside and the consultant asked the owner to meditate and tell the rabbits she was sorry and invite them back. She also said to feed them if they returned and maybe they would not eat the existing plants. They both meditated on it immediately. They went back outside and there was a little rabbit just sitting there looking at them from the corner of the lot. Well, you guessed it. The wild bunnies moved in, and two weeks later, not only was the owner inspired in her career; she took a new job that allowed her to have her own department, which meant more creative freedom, something she had always dreamed about.

Too Much of a Good Thing?

A friend of mine—a fellow feng shui consultant—was desperately trying to have a baby, to no avail. Every time she found out from her fertility specialist that she was not pregnant, she added more enhancements to her Children and Creativity area. She eventually became overwhelmed with the entire process. Another feng shui consultant visited her one day and noticed that my friend had way too many enhancements in the Children section, making it feel out of proportion and balance. "Here's a case of 'Too much of a good thing can be bad for you.'" the consultant said. "This is why you feel overwhelmed." The consultant also noticed that there were fifteen empty containers, from silver teapots to vases and other vessels, in the Children area of the dining room; she suggested filling them up—perhaps with children's things. My friend and her husband wrote out wishes for a child and then placed them inside the containers. She also asked a friend's child to choose some toys to place inside them as well. Within six weeks (after previously spending months working with fertility doctors) she was on her way to motherhood. (As I am writing this, she is pregnant again—no doctors needed.)

If one is good, is twenty better? Not necessarily. Find balance.

Taking a Dip in the Fountain of Youth

Scoot over, alpha hydroxy, there's a new antiaging device in town! It's called *using feng shui in the Children and Creativity zone.* You think I'm kidding, don't you? Well, I'm not. If you crank this area up in your living quarters, you can make a difference in how you age—and it doesn't even need FDA approval!

Do some tests of your own. Observe old people. I'll bet you'll find that the ones who have no hobbies or interests look and act a lot older than the ones who do. OK, forget hobbies for a sec. Think of a person with a defeatist, "Been there, done that" attitude and one with a zest for learning—old, young. Bottom line, you are either soaking up life or withering on the vine. I heard of a study where they took some old people and placed them in an environment that replicated typical surroundings when they were in their twenties—music, decor, and such—and not only did they start to act younger, they actually started regenerating new cells within their physical bodies where they weren't supposed to be able to. These old people were making twenty-year-olds' cells! What a difference an environment makes, huh?

So, if you apply this type of thinking to your feng shui, especially to the Children and Creativity area, you can make a huge difference in how you age. Find a few things that made your heart sing in the past and make a little space for them in the present. Whether it's big band music, Kool-Aid popsicles, or a jump rope, enveloping yourself with such youthful reminders can literally slow down the aging process. I'm not advocating living in the past here, but merely creating surroundings that make you feel alive and youthful.

An Ounce of Prevention

A client, Alexandria, had the Children and Creativity section of her family's new home missing. An outdoor courtyard with a built-in barbecue engulfed their whole Children section. Although the courtyard was to be used as an outdoor play space for their three kids, the ch'i stagnated and eddied. The missing piece created a weakened condition for the home—not to mention the influence of ch'i-melting barbecue! Alexandria asked me to help the family with their landscape design. These were my suggestions:

1. Complete the space by burying a line of red string across the border of the missing piece (see Figure 26).
2. Place plants that bloom white and yellow in planters.
3. Make sure one plant offers a fragrant smell that can enter the house.

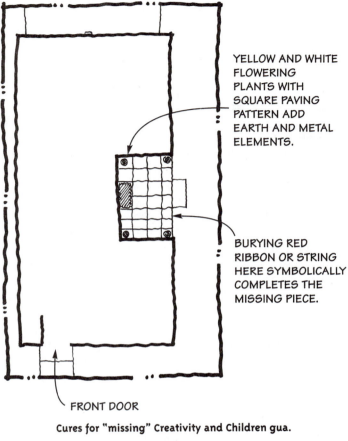

YELLOW AND WHITE
FLOWERING
PLANTS WITH
SQUARE PAVING
PATTERN ADD
EARTH AND METAL
ELEMENTS.

BURYING RED
RIBBON OR STRING
HERE SYMBOLICALLY
COMPLETES THE
MISSING PIECE.

FRONT DOOR

Cures for "missing" Creativity and Children gua.

FIGURE 26

4. Color the concrete an earth-toned color and score it into squares.

So far, so good.

This is only a theory of mine, but I venture to speculate that in homes where children leave too early, run away, or actually become missing, the Children section of the home is physically missing or very poorly feng shuied.

Color Your World—Starting in the Closet

Let's get creative with clothes now.

Each color possesses its own vibration. And with that vibration comes its power. Tap into that power by intentionally wearing specific colors in specific circumstances. Mix and match to get exactly what you want out of life.

Black is mysterious. Black is deep. Black is alluring. Wear black when you are in a reflective mood or wish to focus on your life path. Got Prozac? This color can bring some people down, so do some mood monitoring before wearing black.

Blue has the ability to calm people inside. This is necessary to find internal thoughts—thus the Skills and Knowledge color. Wear it when you meditate. Wear it if you need to have a clear communication with someone (like breaking up or asking for money). Avoid this color if you have the blues.

Green is soothing, something that all families want to feel when together. This color of photosynthesis can bring renewed life to something that appears lifeless and dull. Wear green if you are into "growing" a family or just generally in a community frame of mind. This is also a great healing color.

Purple is the color of nobility. Everyone could use a little purple power. If there are two more days to survive until payday, feel rich and royal anyway by wearing purple.

Red is a very bold statement indeed. It is the color of blood—a strength sign. Wear red in a situation where you need extra power—like when negotiating a raise or buying a car.

Pink reminds us of the blush of a cheek, a softness within the skin, which can bring us to new heights with relationships. Increase romance in your life—cover yourself in pink. Avoid this color in situations where you need power.

White is the universal color because it is really all colors—therefore the color of infinity and endless thought, or creativity. I believe creation was born out of white—not black or darkness, as some wish to think. Wear white to bring order to your creative ideas or excel in higher thoughts.

Gray is between white and black. It is what takes the process from thought to action—thus the color between Creativity and Career. It is the action of creativity. Wear gray if you are in the middle of a project and seek its completion.

Yellow is the color that helps us to focus on the matter at hand—on earth, our temporary residence. Use yellow to get grounded, focus attention, or cheer up.

Children—A Big Part of the Family

It's not too big a stretch to see how the Creativity and Children gua and the Family gua work with each other (see Figure 27). They are opposing guas and can be used all sorts of ways to enhance each other. Picture a defiant child or abusive parent and you can almost too vividly imagine the friction and negative ch'i creating distance in their lives.

Place a physical token with your intention in the Family section to enhance the Creativity and Children gua. Intend that it help you resolve a family squabble or become free of family toil if that is a problem in your life. Also use it if you feel creatively squelched by a family member not allowing your full creative spirit to shine.

Washing Their Mouths with a Bar of Soap

The Children and Creativity part of the home is also associated with the mouth. Be sure to enhance this area of the home if anyone who lives there has sensitive teeth, deteriorating gums, canker sores, or other mouth problems (like bad breath—yuck!)

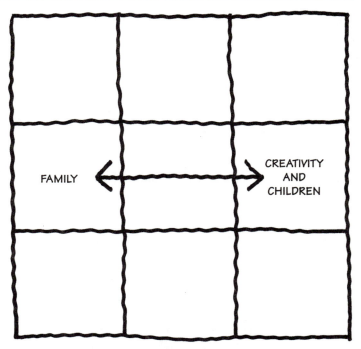

FIGURE 27

Three-Year-Old Thinking

The number 3 carries with it the essence for Creativity and is most closely associated with this area of the home. If you notice, most three-year-olds constantly ask the question "Why?" because they have yet to learn any type of limitation. If you live in this vibration you will find yourself less intimidated by limitations, because of your confidence in formulating a creative solution to life's challenges. Have fun with this one, but check in with reality every once in a while—because "getting too far out there" is the challenge of the 3.

Another way to use these numbers is to place that quantity of power tools in a specific gua to change something in your life. For example, add three metal-framed photos of your kids in the

Creative and Children gua with a specific intention. It just adds another layer to your feng shui enhancements.

Immediate Action Items for Creativity and Children

1. Hang a mirror over any fireplaces.
2. Relocate any candles that are currently in this area (try the Fame or Health zone).
3. Unblock anything that feels blocked or is literally blocked by something else in this gua (doors, drawers, furniture, walkways).
4. Add enhancements as necessary.

Creativity and Children in Summary

Power Tools: metal, white, round stuff, earth, yellow, flat or square stuff, television, toys and games, candy, magic tricks, parties, music, art, hobbies and crafts, bed, lights, bells, symbols of creativity, symbols of children.

Hazardous Materials: fire, red, triangular or pointy objects.

Opposite Gua: Family

Body Part: mouth

Associated Number: 3

chapter 6

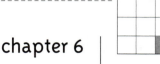

911—Helpful People and Travel

I t's the little things in life that nag with such intensity—like when the dry cleaner loses your dress the day before you need it. Or how about when the guy in the big car steals your parking space—like he didn't see you sitting there patiently waiting with your blinker on. It can blow your whole day.

When these things happen and you get upset, your energy is being used up like a battery in a new toy on Christmas day. These are the flea bites of life—not life threatening, but every once in a while you have to stop what you are doing and scratch. What a distraction. What a loss of valuable energy. Is being treated fairly and honestly really too much to ask? Consider this chapter life's little flea repellant. Help can be available every time you ask if you use the following feng shui secrets.

"Little leaks sink big ships." In other words, it doesn't take much to rob you of energy, and every teeny bit counts.

Help out the Helpful People and Travel area of the home and you'll improve your life the following ways:

- You will find yourself being treated more fairly and honestly.
- You'll find yourself at the right place at the right time more consistently.
- The right people will become more available and willing to help you or teach you.
- Things will run more smoothly.
- Traveling will become less stressful, less chaotic, and more fun.
- Your intuition or divine guidance will become more easily accessible.
- You will get more done because you won't be doing it all yourself.
- Feelings like "If I don't do it, it won't get done" or "It's always up to me" will disappear.

"Helpful people, what's that?" someone said to me. This woman felt like the weight of the world was always on her shoulders every time anything needed to get done. "It's not like I don't have the money to pay people either, because I do. I still can't get good help these days." If you share the sentiment of this woman, chances are the Helpful People and Travel area of your home is not in balance.

Let People Help—It's OK

Some people may not notice there is a problem. Either they have always done everything themselves and don't know any better, or they thrive on the guilt trip they inflict or the approval they get by handling everything themselves. Life is not about going it alone all the time. It is about serving others and allowing others to serve you. Here's a new way of looking at this situation: by going it alone, you are not allowing others to stretch their wings and grow by helping you. Does that make some of you feel any better?

I know all about this condition. I took pride in doing everything myself. I saw allowing others to help as a sign of my own weakness. I would stand on a teetering chair on top of the table to hang blinds rather than ask the neighbor with a ladder for help. Yes, I had discipline. Yes, I was independent. But let me tell you, it sure got lonely, too. And if someone did help me, I felt overly obligated to return the favor. I did not allow them to simply be kind and generous toward me. No, I had to cook up a big meal, throw money in their faces, or mentally keep tally of the favors I owed. I wasn't being kind and generous back—I was desperately trying to keep it even. So, watch out for signs like these, because you are not in the flow with life if you are living like this.

Now, back to those who are doing everything themselves and know it's not fun. There is a spot in the home that can help—get that spot working and people will get working soon thereafter. It is located in the front right corner of your home as you enter through the main door (see Figure 28). Travel to it and see what's there. Compare it to the following list of power tools and hazardous materials, and then you'll know how to avoid your own 911 emergency.

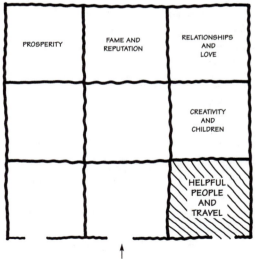

THIS SIDE OF THE BAGUA ALWAYS HAS
THE MAIN DOOR OF THE HOME OR ROOM LOCATED ON IT.

Helpful People and Travel location in bagua.
FIGURE 28

Power Tools for Helpful People and Travel

Silver Containers   Silver works well in this gua. Because this area is next to Creativity and Career, both metal and water are OK here too. My no-frills answer to having silver and metal here is to use aluminum foil.

If you want to set up this corner for life in the most efficient manner, I would suggest the following:

Position three containers for three different tasks of attracting helpful people somewhere in the vicinity (remember, they don't have to be publicly displayed). Optimally, these three should include one small silver box with a lid (real silver, silver-plated, or even a paper box painted silver), one silver envelope large enough to hold documents (from a stationery store, or use an aluminum foil envelope), and one larger container like a paper grocery bag or box (spray it silver if you want).

The small silver box is used for events that need help now (three days to three weeks). This container must have a lid. I prefer those little jewelry boxes with red velvet inside (remember—red can activate something). This container will hold papers with names of people or projects on it. So, for convenience, make the box at least business-card size. As a rule, do not place more than three requests in this container at one time. Here are the requests I currently have in my box as examples:

"Delta Air Lines ticket agents are helpful to me." The counter
    closed before I could purchase the ticket I had reserved, and
    the fare went up. I have to go to the ticket office tomorrow.
"I attract only the perfect health care practitioners for me." I
    am looking for help with my allergies.

The second container is a silver envelope large enough to hold legal-type documents (approximately nine by twelve inches). Stationery stores carry this size of envelope. If it is silver or gray, so much the better. You can also use one of those aluminum foil bags made for cooking. This envelope is used for things that last months (scripts, contracts, invitations). Remember to remove an item when you've been adequately helped.

The third container is for things that stay around for a long time—your doctor, your business clients, your mentors, your family tree. You can essentially place the name of everyone you meet in this container.

The reason I suggest using specific containers is that these three (or however many of these three you need) will remind you what they are for every time you see them. And this reminder is the thought that attracts the helpful energy. Got it?

Gray   The color gray is the best color for this area. As you notice, this gua is located between the Creativity (white) and Career (black) guas, just as the color gray is between white and black.

Any and all stuff that is gray is invited to hang out here to get helpful people in your life (well, except for things like loose gray hairs).

Symbols of Helpful Beings, Religious Objects   Whether human or from another time or dimension, enlist any being as a helpful person by placing a symbol of them here. Place them with the intention of having them help you in life. I've seen pictures of Mother Teresa, Jesus, the Dalai Lama, Martin Luther King Jr., John F. Kennedy, Quan Yin, and the Virgin Mary in this corner. I have seen angel Christmas ornaments used throughout the year here. Dr. Wayne Dyer, Tony Robbins, Laura Schlessinger, and Deepak Chopra have graced this corner by way of their books and tapes, as have the names of preachers and teachers, and business cards of creditors and realtors. Who do you want to help you?

Bells   Think of a polite-sounding bell that rings for service. When you place a bell here, your request will be heard.

Water   Water is a symbol of spirit—good help indeed.

Hands   Helping hands make a fitting embellishment for this space. A simple outline of a hand on paper can be used with the right intention. If you bought one of those battery-operated gag-gift hands for Halloween, maybe you can recycle it in this zone.

Symbols of Favorite Places   If you yearn to travel to a particular place, put a picture of it in this space. It could be a cabin at a nearby lake or an exotic land far away—whatever makes your heart sing when you think of being there.

Hazardous Materials for Helpful People and Travel

Junk   Who wants to hang around in a bunch of junk? Not helpful people. These people are neat freaks. A big ol' mess in this area of the house will give them obstacles to negotiate—thereby taking longer to help you. Clear out that clunky fridge. The scuba tank and spare set of crutches can go too. All pictures that aren't on walls should be in the front yard with a big *Free to a Good Home* sign on them. I'm serious—no junk here.

Drains   If there is a big shower drain in this corner, it not only may be impeding your helpful people from being there, it may be undermining the support you need to prosper. Since this gua is directly opposite the Prosperity area, your abundance is most affected by it. Support and helpful people are usually vital to making money. Even self-made millionaires got a heck of a lot of help from others to get where they are. If Martha Stewart didn't have the great entourage she has, do you think she could pull off all she is accomplishing? If Bill Gates weren't in the right place at the right time and didn't get help from all his employees and other investors, could he really have made that much money? Without people being willing to pay for laughs, could Jim Carrey pull down the big bucks he gets for acting funny? OK, forget millionaires for a sec. Could I be sitting here writing this book if my husband didn't help by paying the bills for a year? Thanks, honey! Sometimes it's good to stop and see where all your help is coming from and trace the road money travels to get to you.

Back to drains. Look closely and see where they may be affecting you in life. Actually, they are not great features anywhere. Be sure to check them out all over the house—it is not just a Helpful People gua problem. If it is a sink drain, tie a red ribbon or red tape around the outgoing pipe (see Figure 29). If it is a shower or floor drain, either use a decorative drain stopper, or get red under the existing stopper (enamel paint sprayed in drain), or keep the drain closed when it is not in use. Also, place mirrors in the area (facing any direction) to keep the ch'i up. These little cures can make a big difference in the flow of ch'i in your home. Everyone can benefit from this simple technique. So, if you are drained of money, friends, lovers, or health, or have any other bad luck, get out the red tape. Hey, and if you are so broke you don't have a buck to spend on tape, go to a dry cleaner and ask them for some. They're usually pretty generous with their red tape and don't even ask questions.

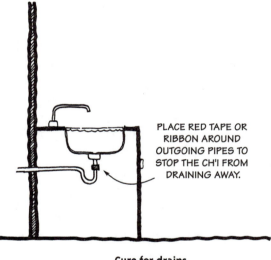

PLACE RED TAPE OR RIBBON AROUND OUTGOING PIPES TO STOP THE CH'I FROM DRAINING AWAY.

Cure for drains.
FIGURE 29

Prosperity Corner Hazardous Materials   All the noxious things mentioned in the hazardous materials list from the Prosperity chapter aren't good here either. To recap them: dirt and dust, broken items, trash cans, toilets, and reminders of being broke or of other bad times. Trash cans and toilets are the only things that you may really need in your house; the rest should go. Make the best of toilets and trash cans, keeping them as clean and pleasant as possible—stinky stuff is no good. Stick up a Stick-Up if you need one.

Get Jacked In—Networking Magic

In business as in many other parts of life, it's not what you know, it's who you know. And it's the who that this part of the home reinforces. Whether it's the best-paying clients or a new lead for a job, working on this part of your home now can save you work later. Any of the above power tool enhancements placed in this area may work, but using a specific person's name can yield very specific results.

Tom knew he was going to get chewed out by his boss for questionable items on his expense report. The boss asked him to show up in the managers' meeting the next day to discuss it. Tom asked my consultant friend Nate what to do. He suggested placing the boss's name in a silver box in his Helpful People corner. He then told Tom that whatever the outcome, it would be fair.

The next day, when Tom went into the meeting, his boss, without question, gave him a bigger expense account.

The reason Nate and I suggest placing specific names here (and in the following examples) is so you focus your attention on the matter you wish to be helped with *and* on the person or persons who can actually help. You could just as easily write a generic affirmation or request specific help for a situation, but if you include a potential helpful person's name, you can achieve better results. It's that ancient Chinese secret from way back—*energy follows thought*—that you're tapping into here. If you think of that person being helpful in your life, you've given the matter that much more energy.

The Dragon Lady

I know a man named Clarence who has a very wealthy but extremely intolerant mother. He affectionately calls her the Dragon

Lady. She called him one day to let him know she was sending him $3,000. He immediately started dreaming about the minivan he wanted to buy. Unfortunately, while he was dreaming, he didn't hear her reason for sending the dough. He went out and bought the van on credit, knowing the money was on its way. Later he called his mother to tell her the news, when to his amazement, she exploded. "Didn't you hear anything I said? That money was supposed to be used for the cruise I planned for the family reunion," she screeched. She then continued, "You are coming to the reunion. I am not sending any more money. Figure it out," and hung up.

Clarence knew he had unleashed the evil forces bubbling deep within her, and fear welled up inside him. He called his feng shui consultant posthaste. He did not want to buy the minivan with his savings. He did not want to give up the van. He did not dare think to miss the reunion. He knew his mother *never* went back on her word, as the sentence "I am not sending you any more money" lingered in his head.

The consultant suggested placing his mother's name inside the silver box in his Helpful People corner. To his total amazement, his mother relented for the first time in her life and called to say she was sending him more money.

Contractors from Hell

If there is one group of people who usually come up in the Helpful People conversation, it's contractors. But unfortunately, they are repeatedly being described as the antithesis of helpful. There's nothing more aggravating than having a big hole ripped in your house and a contractor who, without warning, doesn't show up for days. *Helpless* is the word most used to describe this situation. If you employ the silver box remedy to pick the best contractor, you can turn *helpless* to *helpful*. Allow it to work by opening yourself to the opportunities that start to appear before you—a friend speaks highly of her contractor, or a contractor's truck (complete with a tailgate phone number displayed) is stuck in traffic right in front of you. These events may be your little box at work.

| The Art of Selling Houses, Cars, and Products |

If you are looking for the right person to buy your house, place the business cards of anyone involved in the sale (real estate agent, mortgage lender, appraiser, termite inspector) in the document envelope, along with any contracts, offers, sales fliers, and anything else you have associated with the home sale. Intend for them to help with whatever you need.

If you are trying to sell your car, you can simply write, "The perfect new owner for my car," on a piece of paper and place it in your silver box.

If you sell products for a living, request perfect buyers. They are usually the ones that pay (who needs deadbeats?), like your product (who needs returns?), and tell others how great the product is (helping you sell more). Do this by writing, "I request only good customers for my business (or product)," on a paper and—you guessed it—place it in the box.

If you have sold products or services and the companies or people have not paid within the appropriate time (or worse yet, paid with rubber checks), place their names in the silver box. Because this area is about fairness—and not paying for requested products and services is unfair—this zone can improve your bottom line. If it is just a few offenders, place each of their names on a separate paper in the box. If you consistently have a long-delinquent accounts receivable report each month, you can place the entire list in the box. Don't place names in the box unless their accounts are actually overdue—let nature take its course first. If you request only good customers as stated above, this list should dwindle away.

| Getting Even |

Remember that story awhile back about interviewing for a job with someone equally qualified? Well, what if you were interviewing for a job, had the same qualifications as another applicant, *and* just happened to look just like the boss's evil cousin? Who's going to get the job? (Another example: you have to appear in court before a judge.) Wouldn't it be nice to know you will be treated fairly in such a situation? The well-adorned Helpful People corner of the house virtually negates all bias from individuals when they deal with you.

The Helpful People area of the home is not meant to be used to manipulate people. It is meant only to bring you what is fair. If your intention is to manipulate, the only person who will pay is you.

A Road More or Less Traveled

Some people want to travel more, and some less. Use this part of the house to manifest the right amount of travel for you. Simple enhancements can make this happen.

If you are traveling too much (or too little) for work, enhance your Career area as well. I have seen musicians who make their living on the road suddenly find opportunities to make a better living working in a studio at home. I also know several salespeople who, after pumping up these guas, started to travel more (as they had hoped) to sell their wares.

If you are just a person looking for adventure, use this area to get you there. Arrange a spot with the names or pictures of the places you want to see, and then watch out for the opportunities. Say, for example, you secretly yearn to experience the Siberian high country. You could ever-so-discreetly outfit a closet in the Helpful People and Travel gua with snowshoes, thermal undies, and a book describing how to survive in white-out weather conditions. Then you watch out for hints—either obvious or subtle—that may lead you to your destination.

In my single, more worldly days, I found a way to travel internationally three years in a row—with very little money. People often asked me how I could do it, because I was a sole proprietor without employees. I said, "You just buy a ticket." But really, it was my Helpful People and Travel section working for me. My *will* (intention) provided the *way*. My business volunteered the time when I needed it, and my friends helped with the household upkeep while I was gone. After returning from a trip to Japan, I was called by the international courier service who flew me there (I told you I spent very little money!) to see if I could fly to Hong Kong for free. How often does this happen, I thought!

I also wanted to spend some time in Hawaii. Since I am a landscape architect, I decided to put some of my energy toward getting a license to practice there. That little bit of energy went a long way. I eventually flew over to take the licensing exam. At the testing location, I met an architect from California (also taking the test) who had a hotel project that needed a landscape architect. He said, "If you pass the test, give me a call." Long story short—I got the job and had to go to Hawaii on business five times. Each time I was able to extend the trip a few days so I could tour the islands.

> Sometimes, if you are very clear about your goal, a little initiative can go a long way—even without moving something in your home. Inventory your existing resources, intend for them to serve you in new ways, and use them in new ways as best you can.

Perhaps, if you are not traveling enough for your taste, you should also add a little something to your Creativity area because you may just need to think more creatively about travel.

If you are planning to move (say, because you sold your house or got a new job), activate the Travel gua for a safe trip. You should know the routine by now.

Wishing You the Best

If you can't think of anything specific that you need help with, or you have already employed the above wisdom and no longer have any complaints, you can simply reinforce this spot with an affirmation to keep the helpful energies invigorated. Write something like "I am always in the right place at the right time" or "I travel the perfect amount" or "There is always someone there to help when I need them" on pieces of paper and place them in your silver box. You can change the affirmations, or just read them every once in a while to reinforce them.

First Class Taste on Coach Budget

If you want to upgrade yourself into traveling first class, enhance the gua opposite Helpful People and Travel—the Prosperity gua (see Figure 30). With the right stuff placed with the right intention, you can say good-bye to motor lodges and peanuts and say hello to the Ritz and chocolate soufflé.

Headin' Out

The body part connected to the Helpful People and Travel area of the home is the head. If your noggin needs repair, give this corner a little care.

Five Countries in a Day

The Helpful People and Travel part of the house is connected to the 5 vibration. Like your fingers, 5 is a handful. If you are up to globe-trotting and are looking forward to what tomorrow may bring, a 5 home is for you. If you are not up to spontaneous parties or unusual adventures and you live in a 5 house, pack your bags.

Immediate Action Items for Helpful People and Travel

1. Create a place to house your requests for helpful people (with aluminum foil or silver containers).
2. Add enhancements as necessary.

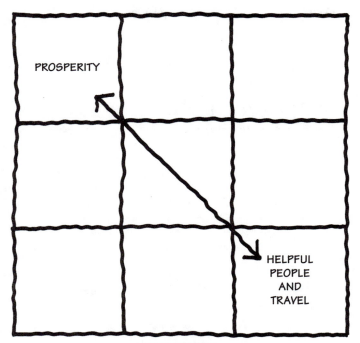

FIGURE 30

| Helpful People and Travel in Summary |

Power Tools: silver containers, gray, symbols of helpful beings, religious objects, bells, water, hands, symbols of favorite places.

Hazardous Materials: junk, drains, dirt and dust, broken items, trash cans, toilets, reminders of broke and bad times.

Opposite Gua: Prosperity
Body Part: head
Associated Number: 5

chapter 7

At the Intersection of Possibility and Potential—Career and Life Path

Following the feng shui path in the Career area of the home can create results. You can

- get a job
- get a new, better, or more meaningful job
- enjoy your work
- have business pick up
- make more money in business
- figure out what you want to do with your life and do it—as in "Follow your heart"

Did you win the lottery or that big, million-dollar sweepstakes this week? Well, if not, then you are probably still going to work every day. Hey, we all have to work, but we also have the luxury of choice. You have the freedom to choose something else if you aren't really into what you're currently doing. Choice equals change. And change is the only thing that's certain in life.

When it comes to traveling on your life path, are you stopped at a red light? Is your life path filled with potholes? Are you stuck in gridlock and there's no exit in sight? Well, pull over

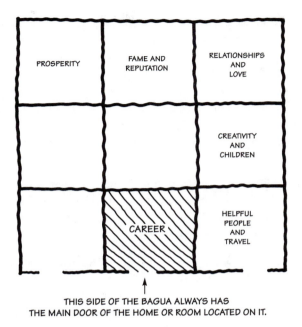

THIS SIDE OF THE BAGUA ALWAYS HAS
THE MAIN DOOR OF THE HOME OR ROOM LOCATED ON IT.

Career location in bagua.
FIGURE 31

and read on, because this is your twenty-four-hour roadside assistance program.

Take the first step on your life path by going immediately to the front door. As you walk through, find the center of the wall plane that the door is on, because the Career section is front and center in the home (see Figure 31). It is directly opposite the Fame and Reputation gua in the rear of the home. Now that you know where it is, it's easy to bring about change. Both kinds—cha ching!

Power Tools for Career and Life Path

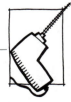

Plug in some of these tools in the Career area of your home:

Water   Although most people think the only qualified water for this section is a fountain, an aquarium, or a river, it really can be any kind of water (as long as it's not smelly toilet water). That's why so many Chinese restaurants have aquariums near the entry. A vase of good clean water will do—you don't need to run the old Slip N' Slide down the hallway.

Symbolic water can work too. A snowy scene in a picture, or even a watercolor of just about anything, invites change (except earth pictures).

Items connected to water also work well here, like starfish or seashells.

Black   Not only is this color just downright cool, it is also the feng shui symbol for water. Throw that black briefcase over there and make it work for you. Or grab that *Men in Black* poster and hang it in the Career section.

Undulating Shapes   The shape or form for the element of water is free-form or undulating. Since water can take on any shape, any shape will do to describe it. The only shape that would be least appropriate would be squares. Square shapes relate to the element of earth, and once again, we don't want earth symbols in this area damming our water.

Mirrors   They also equal water and they let you see how fabulous you look dressed for your new career. In addition, they bounce the light, which keeps energy flowing in this area of the home. Always be careful how you hang a mirror. Make sure it is placed at a level where you can look yourself in the eye and see your entire head. That way you'll get ahead in business.

Mirrors not recommended: those found in fun houses.

Glass   Glass is considered a water element in feng shui. Glass is also used quite extensively in containers for water—vases,

Forget what you've heard about seven years of bad luck—if a mirror breaks, it just means you need a bigger mirror.

aquariums, fish bowls, stemware—so it is usually quite easy to make glass work for your career.

Metal   If you remember from the Creative Cycle in Chapter I (Figure 3), metal "creates" water. So, if you have anything made of metal that would aesthetically work in this area, put it here. Metal of any kind will do, from a brass doorknob to a copper fish fountain. Dig out that photo of yourself wearing braces in the seventh grade and proudly display it here (just kidding).

White Stuff   The color white symbolizes the metal that creates water. Anything that is white will attract good vibes for your life path. Since black and white are the two best colors here, try to find a way to incorporate them into something that makes meaningful sense about what you want to do in life. Books have black-and-white pages, so if you have a book that talks about your career path, try placing it here and see what happens. Race car drivers—a black-and-white checker flag would be awesome here.

Round Stuff   Since round is metal in feng shui, it works well here for your career. Use round metal stuff and cover both bases—coins, bells, plant pots, light fixtures. Handcuffs, medieval weapons, and helmets—probably not.

Symbols of the Life Path You Want to Be On   If your goal is to be a stockbroker, then a picture of Wall Street can work. Or just keep a current copy of the *Wall Street Journal* nearby. If you dream of a career in the music industry, then pipe some music into this area (using it literally) or, symbolically, place instruments, CDs, or posters of recording artists here. If you are in school or your best path in life is not yet clear to you, place items here displaying your current interests, as well as your schoolbooks, with the intention that they help you find the path in life that makes your heart sing. Although I said cures don't have to be showing to be working, in this case, I think overtly surrounding yourself with reminders of your current interests may garner stronger ch'i for you.

Hazardous Materials for Career and Life Path

These are the things that don't help the Career cause:

Dirt   This is not the place for dirt, because when you mix dirt and water you get mud. Even pictures of mountains and clay pots can muddy the water. Keep the water pure.

Squares   Since the square represents earth, and the earth is made of dirt, yadda, yadda, yadda, you get it . . . no squares.

Earth-Tone-Colored Items   Yellows, oranges, and browns—if they are here, try to find a new spot for them.

OK, so you have a yellow square ceramic pot filled with brown dirt and a plant sitting right smack dab in the middle of this zone, and you like it. Don't freak out. It can stay. But if it does, it would be wise to counterbalance the whole area with some of the power tools listed above. And remember, you can also use the Destructive Cycle to your advantage. A big tree in the pot (remember, wood uproots earth) would start to negate the earth element and its power over water.

Here's another example. If you rent an apartment that has bright yellow linoleum squares on the Career section's floor and you can't do anything about it, just make sure you balance the area with something else that works from a design standpoint. I would recommend green items because green is the color for wood, and wood destroys earth. (Review these two cycles—Figures 3 and 4 in Chapter I—if you are still confused.) If you have a large piece of wooden furniture in this area, it will surely start to overcome the power of the yellow. White or metal items, symbolizing the metal element, which makes water, may fit the decor.

Pictures of Things That You Would Never Want to Do in Your Life   In the entry area of a man's home, I saw a black-and-white picture of a tightrope artist walking between two rooftops. Although it was interesting and did make a statement, it created a type of tension within me. The home owner said he really didn't know why, but he hung that picture in his entry every time he moved. He also agreed that his career has always been a great source of tension in his life. (He had the black-and-white thing going for him, but the symbolism outweighed the colors.)

Notebook check. How's that list of existing power tools to use and existing conditions to change coming along for this gua?

The Secret Door to Success Shouldn't Stick

Since the entrance of the room or home is often associated with Career, let's talk about the entry for a bit. Does your entrance seem to mimic your career path? Are there obstacles to negotiate? Does the door stick, and does that echo how you feel about your job? Do you always use another door to enter your house, even though this is the main front door? This may imitate how you are overlooked at work. As crazy as it sounds, the happier your entry, the happier you are with your career or path in life. Keep the entry clean and inviting. Make sure the doorbell works and that there is enough light to feel safe. Be sure nothing is in the way to step over or around when approaching the front door or right after entering the home. (Some of you may remember Dick Van Dyke tripping over the ottoman in the beginning of his television show. He definitely needed a feng shui consultation.) Make your address easy to find and read, and make sure it can't be confused with other addresses, if you are in a multifamily building. Also, make sure the numbers don't go down (see Figure 32).

The front door should reflect authority as well as be inviting. Look at your front door from the street and make sure it is not cowering behind a tree or another object. If you have a double door, do not block one of the doors with potted plants or other objects, or you are blocking half of your ch'i (see Figure 32).

If you feel you need protection, and foo dogs or a convex mirror don't fit your style (they are very traditional Chinese cures), find something that does. Bum some of those little green

DON'T BLOCK YOUR CH'I
BY BLOCKING ANY PART OF
YOUR ENTIRE FRONT DOOR.

HANG ADDRESS NUMBERS LEVEL.
DON'T HANG NUMBERS
GOING DOWN LIKE THIS.

WELCOME

How not to set up the entrance to your home.

FIGURE 32

toy soldiers from the kid next door and hide them in potted plants on both sides of the door. There's nothing like army men guarding a door to keep you safe. Choose something that you would like to have protect you, maybe a concrete dog statue or a pair of topiary lions.

Paint your front door red (or shades of red) if you want feng shui protection. Also use this treatment if you have something negative pointing toward your home, like a road or a corner of a building (see Figure 33). If you are feng shuiing a room only, like a dorm room, painting the door red would be appro-

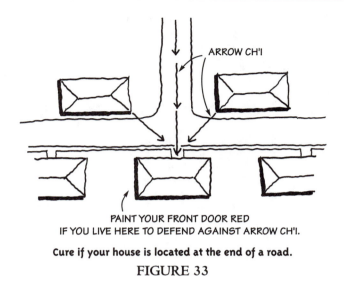

PAINT YOUR FRONT DOOR RED
IF YOU LIVE HERE TO DEFEND AGAINST ARROW CH'I.

Cure if your house is located at the end of a road.

FIGURE 33

priate if your door is at the end of a long hall (see Figure 34). Paint over the red with a landlord-approved color if you must— it's OK. The red and your intention will still be there working for you.

If there are steps to climb near the front door, make sure there is enough room to back up without falling down the stairs if the door opens outward. You don't want to knock the Girl Scouts off the stoop on cookie delivery day.

If you always enter through the garage, and your front door gets little use other than by the occasional trick-or-treater on Halloween, exercise the energy by routinely opening the front door and giving it a little workout. You don't want weak, sleepy, shriveled-up energy inhabiting your home anywhere, even in a space not often used.

Stuck doors make stuck ch'i. Make sure every door opens freely and that all hardware is working. Do not store anything behind a door that would keep it from being opened all the way. Wash the door and the knob regularly.

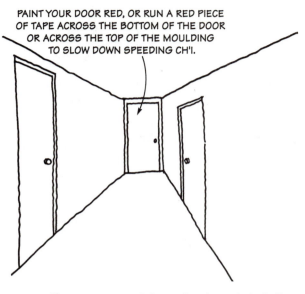

PAINT YOUR DOOR RED, OR RUN A RED PIECE
OF TAPE ACROSS THE BOTTOM OF THE DOOR
OR ACROSS THE TOP OF THE MOULDING
TO SLOW DOWN SPEEDING CH'I.

Cure if your apartment is located at the end of a hall.

FIGURE 34

Now, take a look at what happens once you enter the door-way. Is it scary, confusing, depressing, cluttered, dreary, claustrophobic, or hazardous? No one wants to be greeted in a home with these kinds of spaces. It's best to have enough room for guests to enter, take off a coat, or set down the big presents they may bring. If your entry can't accommodate these functions and you run into a wall as soon as you come into the house, hang a big mirror on the wall that crowds the space. This will give the illusion of a bigger entry. And mirrors, being a water symbol, usually make a good addition to places along the front of the home anyway.

If, upon entering, you see straight through the house and out the back door, you have another kind of ch'i problem: the ch'i is flowing in the front and immediately out the back. The goal is to have it stay awhile. A traditional cure would be to hang a crystal somewhere between the two doors in question (as I suggested you do between the stairs and door, in Chapter 2).

Another idea is to carefully place items to create a meandering path between the two doors (without creating clutter, of course!). This cure holds true when entering any door in the house.

Poinsettias and Professions

My friend recently had a baby and decided to stay home to raise him. She was a little freaked about the loss of her income and wondered how it would affect the household financial situation. Although her husband had a fantastic job, it would definitely put a crimp in the cash flow.

Preparing for the holidays, she decided to trim back the dormant trees and shrubs (which were mostly in the Prosperity and Fame sections of their lot) and to replace the tired seasonal-colored annuals with poinsettia plants in front of the house, leading to the door (Career area). Within a week, her husband was called by a long-time acquaintance to see if he knew of anyone interested—or was interested himself—in a new vice president position for a Las Vegas megacorporation. The perks and pay offered were more than the couple's combined prebaby income.

Trimming the trees and shrubs allowed more ch'i to flow in and around Prosperity and Fame. Clearing out the withered annuals and replacing them with the red poinsettias livened up and activated Career. Without thinking much about it, she had enhanced the precise three places to stir up ch'i for a new, higher-paying job. Activate Prosperity for more money, Fame for shining brightly in the universe and getting noticed, and Career for creating a job worthy of your time while on earth.

With that kind of luck, I think, Las Vegas is a perfect place for this family to live!

Stressed-Out Landscape

As long as I'm talking about the yard, I'll make another observation. I have noticed that when front yards are meticulously and tediously wrought with items like little circles of colored gravel around goofy little statues or topiary, it's usually a sign that there are Life Path issues with the occupants inside. I'm not talking about the well-maintained garden, but a highly controlled "statement" garden, one that looks like a cry for help. For some reason, it seems the more uptight and controlled the landscape looks, the more out of control the person is inside—as if he takes out on his yard his unhappiness and feelings of being controlled. Usually it's the person's career that is out of control. He has a controlling boss or a rigid schedule, or has unreasonable goals placed upon him.

This is a classic Career bagua case for the feng shui consultant. Inside, the Career gua usually has similar signs of distress. If you can relate to this, don't frizz out yet. Just keep reading. Sometimes it is a slow process, but if you follow the wisdom of this book, you will eventually get where you want to be on your life path.

The First Step on the Path

If you are stuck, even when attempting to take the first step on your path, don't worry. Here are two great ways to gather the ch'i to start:

1. Place some uncooked rice in a bowl. Take all the miscellaneous change you accumulate each day and place it in the bowl. Do this for thirty days. After that, count up all the change. Then give 10 percent of it to a charity or a homeless person.

2. Write down the things you think you want out of life, or the things you think you need to begin a career, on pieces of paper—one item per paper. Fold up the papers and place them in a bowl, and stir them with a big spoon or your hand each day for nine days. All of your intentions and requests that once did not have any ch'i

behind them will now be enlivened and start to work for you because you are stirring them up.

It may sound weird, but it's the truth, plain and simple.

Take This Job and Love It

In addition to implementing the above power tools for your Career area, here are things you can do if you are looking for a new job. Hang metal chimes or a bell outside the door to bring attention to yourself. Hang them on the nonhinged side of the door frame. Go to the Helpful People corner (see Chapter 6) and place a piece of paper that says, "The perfect career opportunity," in a silver box (an aluminum-foil-covered box works too). Reinforce this with any affirmations or rituals you like (see Chapter 12), and then your only job is to make sure you look over every opportunity that comes your way. Erase the picture of a specific company from your mind and replace it with a picture of yourself being very happy doing something that you love and collecting a big check for it. Sometimes you have to have one door closed to make room for another to open. So don't panic if you somehow unexpectedly lose your present job. You can't put a new Kenneth Cole shoe on your foot if you keep that ol' Payless shoe strapped to it!

Skipping Rungs on the Corporate Ladder

Say you've got a job you are happy with but you want to advance in the company a little faster. What do you do? Start by attaining what is usually necessary to get a promotion.

Number one: a good reputation. When the corporate commanders think of you, they should think of one thing only—*a great employee.* Your reputation cannot be tarnished. So let's shine it up. Go to the Reputation section and make sure all is well there (see Chapter 3). You can add a little something extra with the intention of making that item help you acquire or keep a good reputation. Light a red seven-day candle and add a new green plant to the area. If you want your employers to think you can do anything, take a picture or poster of your favorite superhero, paste your photo over their face, and put your company name or logo on your chest. Place this somewhere in the Fame and Reputation section and see what happens.

Number two: you need a boss that is going to do something about your career. Write all the names of the decision makers in the company down on paper or company stationery. Add your name to it and place it in the Helpful People corner (see Chapter 6.) If you feel that you do not have a good relationship with one or more of the decision makers, place their names in the Relationship corner too (see Chapter 4), preferably on pink paper. The Relationship corner can help with all relationships, not just ones with lovers.

Remember, it is not necessary to boldly display your cures to the world. Place them behind pictures or in boxes, or tape them under a table in the area. As long as you know they are there, they will work. No one else has to know!

King or Queen of the Cubicle

Stuck in cubicle hell? Let's try to make it livable. Apply the same nine guas to your cubicle as you have to your home, using the entry into the cubicle as the front door. Don't forget that you can feng shui your desk too. (See Figure 13, Chapter 3.) Decorate each area with powerful symbols. Hang a calendar of waterfalls in the Career section. Books should go in the Skills and Knowledge area. Plants are best in the Family or Reputation section but work just about anywhere. A symbol of anything that has great value to you goes in the Prosperity corner. Spouse or lover photos work well in the Relationship corner, and kids (yours or someone else's) next to them in Creativity. Place your Rolodex or handheld computerized address book in the Helpful People area. And finally, tape a construction-paper yellow sun under the middle of the desk for health, and you've got it all.

As with the example of the yellow sun, it may be easier to just use pieces of paper in the correct colors for each area. Cut them in the bagua shape (six inches across will do) for added symbolism and power. Stick them under your desk and you've got one cranked-up cubicle.

If your back is to the door of the cubicle or office when you sit at your desk and there is no way to change that, place a small mirror on your desk in front of you so as to catch a reflection if someone is behind you. Try a rearview mirror from an auto parts supply or a cosmetic case mirror stuck to your computer monitor. If a mirror seems too out of place, use a silver vase, a stainless steel pencil sharpener, or any other shiny, reflective office object.

Ancient Tech Meets High Tech

Since computers, scanners, and printers adorn most offices, you may be wondering if there is a better or worse location for them in your office or cubicle. Although there really is no terrible position for them, you may benefit if they are placed in the bagua area of the office or desk that corresponds to their function. For example, if you trade stocks on a computer all day for a living, then the Prosperity corner would be the way to go. If you use your computer more for its customer tickler file, try Helpful People. If it is used solely for payroll or accounting, perhaps the Family section may be appropriate. And if you are writing a book or screenplay, how about placing it in Fame?

Need more examples? If you are a designer and draw on the computer all day, the Creativity area seems most appropriate. Running a dating service? The computer in the Relationship corner might be the best matchup. I think you get it by now.

If you want to generate more incoming calls (maybe you are in sales), tie a red ribbon around the cord that runs from the jack to your phone. Do it to the modem line if you get business that way too. Want to really pump it up? Tie nine red ribbons instead of just one. Get ready to hear the sound of business ringing in.

Want to pump up the Career feng shui for more business? Meet nine new people for nine or twenty-seven days and see what business comes out of it. Yes, nine people each day who you've never talked to before. Maybe it's a person waiting in line behind you at the dry cleaners. Maybe it's the copy repair person at the office. Introduce yourself and see where it goes. It's pretty much a sure thing to generate new business or some other relationship that can help you in the future.

| Left, Right, Up, or Down? |

If you are looking for direction in your life, or are scattered because you are overwhelmed with all the possibilities and choices, check your shoes. They are the "rubber meeting the road" when it comes to your getting anywhere. Arrange them in the closet so they are all facing the same direction.

If coming out of the closet is a part of your life path, make sure the shoes are facing out, and keep the door ajar until you have succeeded. I would also suggest adding enhancements in the Family and Relationship areas with the specific intention of making this process an enjoyable and loving one.

If you can't picture your goal clearly in your mind and don't know where you are going, it's impossible to know which way to turn, or if you are indeed "there." But when you know where you are going, you not only realize when you have arrived, you can choose the kind of roads you want to take. You can use dangerous cliffside footpaths, meandering slow-paced scenic trails, or the freeway. You will be in charge of your destiny. So get clear on where you want to go. Enhance Skills and Knowledge if you are stuck with this (see Chapter 8).

Retail Rescue

Most businesses that rely on walk-in patronage need lively energy to keep sales flowing. If this is you, here's a tip. Take the merchandise off the shelves (especially slow-moving stuff) and dust the shelf. People don't like to buy dusty stuff anyway. But more important, this will stir up the energy. Stirred-up energy creates sales. As an example, think of all the cheap, hokey stuff car dealers do to catch your attention. They use whirligigs on antennas, strings of flapping pennants, and huge balloons, just to name a few. And they must be getting results or they wouldn't keep doing it. It works because quite simply, it is good feng shui.

If there is a particular part of the store that seems sluggish, enhance it with one of the traditional cures, like a chime above the merchandise, or mirrors behind the shelves. If the whole store is suffering, check the lighting (darkness slows sales), the entry (it's hard to make sales if they can't find you), and your register placement (prominent position seen upon entering, but not too close to the door to tempt robbers). Don't forget about the chime-by-the-door trick that I explained earlier.

Flower Power

In between your home and office is an assortment of spaces and conditions that may be either positively or negatively affecting you. So think about applying feng shui to them to keep your ch'i uplifted. Use my colored construction paper method to feng shui your car (see Figure 35). Cut a six-inch bagua shape in each of the eight outside gua colors and cut a nine-inch circle in yellow for the center. Arrange them in the proper order and tape them together. The final configuration should look like a colorful daisy with a yellow center and different-colored petals. Place this daisy under the mat of the car. The black petal of the daisy should be closest to the rear trunk, and red (Fame) toward the engine. Cut out tiny daisies and place them under your bike seat if that is your mode of transportation. If you ride a train or

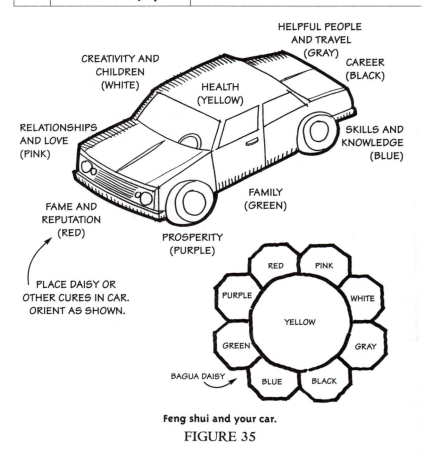

Feng shui and your car.
FIGURE 35

plane to work, simply having a daisy (any size) somewhere on you (or in your briefcase, shoe, or underwear) will assist you while on the road. Since this daisy is a complete bagua representation, it's hard to think of any place inappropriate.

Dipping Your Pen in Company Ink

Just as there is a close connection between your career and your reputation, there is a connection with them in the bagua (see Figure 36). Picture them balancing each other like two kids on

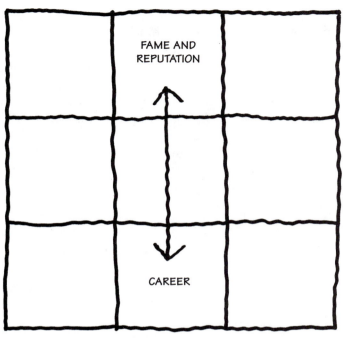

FIGURE 36

a seesaw. If one kid is heavier, the other's feet never gets to touch the ground. Or if one kid gets off, the other plummets to the ground. Likewise with your career. If you build a reputation that is heavy with rumor, negligence, or apathy, you may find it hard to keep your feet on your chosen path due to being fired, laid off, or transferred to a distant land. You don't have to read too far inside the newspapers to find out where sleeping your way to the top gets you. Keep the Career and the Reputation guas in balance to best benefit your career.

An Ear for Career

Children with chronic ear infections? The Career area is associated with the ear. Enhance this area of the bagua if you or someone living in the household is experiencing ear problems.

Six of One, Half a Dozen of Another

Six is the number associated with the Career and Life Path area of the home. The essence of 6 is service. Whether you are a Jelly Belly maker or a jelly-loving belly dancer, your life path includes service—service to your family, other people, the environment, or animals. But being of service is easier to accomplish if you live in a 6 house. One tip for the 6 dweller: be sure to allow receiving in your life, too, because sometimes sixes just give, give, give. If you have six of something in this spot of the house, intend for it to assist with your life path.

Immediate Action Items for Career and Life Path

1. Make sure the front door doesn't stick and opens all the way (nothing stored behind it).
2. Add enhancements as necessary.

Career and Life Path in Summary

Power Tools: water, black, undulating shapes, mirrors, glass, metal, white, round stuff, symbols of life path you want to be on.

Hazardous Materials: dirt, squares, earth-tone colors, pictures of things you would never want to do in your life.

Opposite Gua: Fame and Reputation

Body Part: ear

Associated Number: 6

chapter 8

If I Only Had a Brain— Skills and Knowledge

Placing items wisely in the Skills and Knowledge area of the home could help you

- ⊙ make better grades
- ⊙ make better decisions
- ⊙ be more creative
- ⊙ be a better businessperson
- ⊙ attract opportunities, situations, and people to help in all areas of your life
- ⊙ tap into your inner wisdom more often
- ⊙ find the inner strength and will to begin a seemingly ominous or overwhelming task
- ⊙ have better relationships

If you could feng shui one area of your home, this should be the one. I know, you're probably thinking, "Skills and Knowledge. I've got bigger fish to fry over in Prosperity land. Don't be bothering me with that tired old Skills and Knowledge stuff. My brain isn't on drugs. I'm not so bad off." But trust me, what I'm telling you is true.

Although this area is glossed over by many feng shui practitioners because of its relatively unglamorous title and seemingly unimportant life situation, Skills and Knowledge is vitally important. Our ability to think, rationalize, and purposefully hone our minds is what separates us from all other creatures on earth. Life is a learning process, and the more smarts you have, the better off you'll be. Many feng shui practitioners simply call this bagua area *wisdom*.

Let's say, for example, that you are griping about not having enough money. You start adorning your Prosperity zone with all the right stuff. The money starts to show up. Now, if you don't have your head screwed on right and aren't wise to what's going on, you may not even notice that more money is coming in. Or you may spend it unwisely—thus never feeling prosperous, and thinking feng shui is not working in your Prosperity area.

Or else you amplify the Relationship section because you are looking for the perfect mate. All these people start to show up in your life, but as usual, you choose the losers and completely miss noticing the right one. You don't learn from your own mistakes.

If you don't have the wisdom to make proper choices, you may never even recognize the opportunities and the abundance right in front of you. The term *wisdom* means more than just knowing a lot of facts. I know plenty of people who know tons of stuff, and they still make incredibly poor choices in life. Wisdom is an insightful understanding of what is right, appropriate, or true. With wisdom you can more easily accumulate the things you want out of life—and hey, that's what this is all about, right?

OK, to get to this important corner, go through the main door and turn left. This space to the left of the Career gua in front of the home is considered the Skills and Knowledge gua (see Figure 37). How *smart* does it look?

Sometimes the doorway is located in that corner and you actually enter immediately into Skills and Knowledge. Either way, here's the stuff that works and the stuff that doesn't in this area.

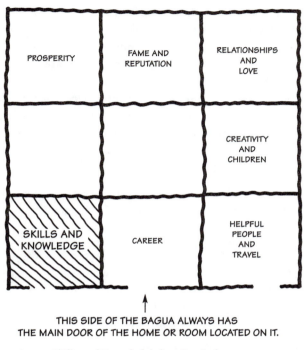

PROSPERITY	FAME AND REPUTATION	RELATIONSHIPS AND LOVE
		CREATIVITY AND CHILDREN
SKILLS AND KNOWLEDGE	CAREER	HELPFUL PEOPLE AND TRAVEL

THIS SIDE OF THE BAGUA ALWAYS HAS
THE MAIN DOOR OF THE HOME OR ROOM LOCATED ON IT.

Skills and Knowledge location in bagua.
FIGURE 37

Power Tools for Skills and Knowledge

Blue   Blue is the color for this part of the bagua, so just about anything blue will do. Cramming for finals? Hang your blue jeans in the corner to get a better grade. Viagra is a little blue pill. Blue is for *skills* and knowledge. Hmmm . . .

Books   Books make the perfect enhancement for the Skills and Knowledge area, for obvious reasons. Use a few or all you've got. Even if this area falls in your garage, set up a little spot to display stuff that helps you get wise. Use bookends that symbolize a skill of yours, or a skill that you would like to master. A friend of mine has his books held up by blue polished geode bookends. He's into geology among other things.

Light   Light is one of those traditional cures that can energize just about anything. But used here in the Skills and Knowledge section, it can be especially meaningful. Any light works great—lamps with lightbulbs, lanterns, candles. Heck, just a lightbulb with proper intent can do the trick. The sayings "Shed some light on the subject" and "Gain enlightenment" hint that light helps with knowledge and intelligence. If you are using a lamp, remember—as long as it is plugged in and works, it will do. It does not have to be on for good feng shui.

Food   If your kitchen is in this corner of your home, intend that all the food you buy become food for thought. (Who would have thought Cap'n Crunch and lamb chops could be so useful?)

Things That Remind You of Wisdom   A replica of Rodin's *The Thinker,* a lamp of knowledge, the scales of justice, a judge's gavel, a chess game, a straight-A report card, and those cute, intelligent dolphins all make great ch'i enhancers. If you think higher thoughts with something, put it here.

Symbols of Mentors or Wise People   A statue of Solomon would make a great symbol of wisdom. He was the guy in the Bible that, when God asked him what he wanted, responded, "Wisdom." He knew that if he had wisdom he could get the other stuff—money, land, health, and anything else he needed.

You can also use the three Wise Men (even if it's not Christmas), Merlin the magician, Yoda, Ben (Obi-Wan) Kenobi, Einstein, or Gandhi depicted in statues, pictures, posters, or toys.

Metal   "Sharp as a tack" and "razor-sharp mind" help illustrate how metal can suggest great intelligence. Remember the "one-cent cure"—a penny? It's metal and it has Lincoln on it, who is known for his intelligence and wisdom. "A penny for your thoughts!" Save your pennies here and see what thoughts come of it.

Water   Borrowing the water from next door in Career can enliven this gua to invite wisdom your way. From a little bud vase to a hot tub, start the waterworks and get into the "stream" of consciousness.

Black   As long as you can use water, you can use the color that symbolizes the element. Nuns, priests, Quakers, and Shakers— hang your black garb here.

Wood   Borrow the element from the gua on the other side, Family. Wood works well placed intentionally to attract wisdom. All that paper in those books is trees in action.

Green   Wood and green—same thing in feng shui. Use green plants, dollar bills, clothes, or paint—anything green.

Meditation Items   If you find your wisdom by meditating, this area of the home will yield the best insights. Create a quiet retreat using your bench, chair, or pillows.

Altars of Thanksgiving   Creating a small place in this gua to remind you of all the things you have to be thankful for can add to your wisdom and awareness.

Symbols of the Skills or Knowledge You Want to Have   College students, put things here that symbolize your major. (And while you're working on this, consider removing the collection of beer bottles from around the world.) Hobbyists, work your craft here.

Hazardous Materials for Skills and Knowledge

Clutter   Thinking clearly requires a clear space. Don't clutter your mind with unnecessary stuff in your living quarters . . . and yes, I mean the whole house.

Things That Stop the Thought Process   Alcohol, drugs, poisons, and cigarettes all cloud the thought process and should be kept away from here. If you happen to have a bar in this area of your home, balance it out by having some healthy choices to offer guests—perhaps a juice bar and alcohol bar combo. Sorry about those cigs, smokers, but it really is not too wise to smoke, even if it makes you relax so you can think.

Remember, you have to do your part. Feng shui will only meet you halfway. If you get bombed every night and blow off your job or homework, all the gua embellishing in the world isn't going to lead you to wisdom or happiness.

Unwise Symbols Be careful with the newspaper—it is chock full of stupid people and stupid things (corruption, murder, fires, bankruptcies), things you don't want to invite into your life. Mike Tyson, Bill Clinton or Monica Lewinsky, River Phoenix, Robert Downey Jr., or anyone else who has done something stupid or just doesn't get it needs to stay out of this zone.

Left Your Brain in the Garage?

In a lot of homes, the Skills and Knowledge or Helpful People area of the house falls in the garage. As much as some people hope that their garage is not a part of their home, if it lies behind the plane of the front door, it is (see Figure 38). Now, don't go running off to sue your architect or builder yet. Most are oblivious to feng shui. I'm sure they didn't do it intentionally. (Support the feng shui cause—give an architect a copy of this book!)

Garages have an unusual energy about them. Either they have very fast energy whirling about from vehicles coming and going, or they are so crammed with junk that the cars don't fit, and the energy has come to a grinding, stagnating halt. Either way, the energy is not suitable for comfortable living.

Here's what you can do about it:

1. Cut the crap. You've got to take a stand against storing stuff you simply don't use very often. The more clutter you have, the more brainpower you use subconsciously keeping track of it. Clear the clutter and you clear your mind. I will give a generous exception to the following if they are carefully organized and not overdone: holiday

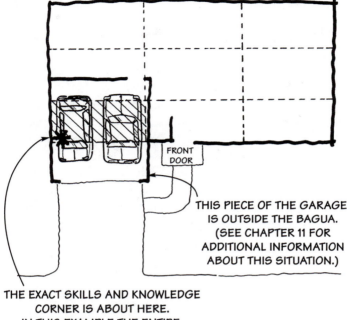

THIS PIECE OF THE GARAGE
IS OUTSIDE THE BAGUA.
(SEE CHAPTER 11 FOR
ADDITIONAL INFORMATION
ABOUT THIS SITUATION.)

THE EXACT SKILLS AND KNOWLEDGE
CORNER IS ABOUT HERE.
IN THIS EXAMPLE THE ENTIRE
SKILLS AND KNOWLEDGE GUA
FALLS IN THE GARAGE.

Garage in Skills and Knowledge gua.
FIGURE 38

decorations (unless it's scary, bloody Halloween gunk); children's clothing and toys (if you are waiting for a younger sibling to grow into them); papers (the ones the IRS makes you keep for so many years).

And after you have the crap out, clean the garage as if it is a room in the house. Sweep the floors and dust away the spiderwebs.

2. Clean your cars. If your car is filled with stale french fries and cigarette butts, you can't help but have grubby energy around you. And if this skanky car is sitting in your wisdom area, well, what does that say about how smart you are? Besides affecting your Skills and Knowledge, a dirty car affects many other areas of life as well. Sit among the burger wrappers and big-gulp cups in a grungy car and then sit in a freshly detailed car, and tell me you can't feel the difference. You wear this difference the way the car does. Think about that before you go to a job interview in a sloppy, sticky car.

3. Lube the door. Entering your home by way of a squeeky, creepy, clunky garage door opening does not make for the perfect welcoming experience. "Stuck doors make stuck ch'i" applies to garage doors too.

4. Shed some light. Garages without windows can appear quite dank inside. Make sure each corner is filled with an appropriate amount of light. No room in your home—even the garage—should creep you out.

The Wisdom to Go It Alone

My friend and feng shui practitioner Nate went to the home of a bachelor doctor who asked for his help. Although the doctor was prosperous and had money, he felt he didn't know enough to decorate or properly furnish his home. One quick look around and Nate could see he was right. The home had the signature of a poor college student—boxes for shelves, hodge-podge furniture, and no window treatments. The doctor wanted Nate to help him "decorate" his home.

Since Nate prides himself on feng shui and not necessarily interior design, he simply activated two areas of the bagua and left it at that. The two areas were Skills and Knowledge and Creativity. Nate explained that these two areas would help the doctor get the knowledge he needed to complete this task and confidence in his decision making. Nate also explained that enhancing the Creativity area would unearth the doctor's long-since-squelched creative side, and help him with decorating ideas. Nate left the doctor to his own devices.

About two months later, the doctor asked Nate over to see the place. When Nate entered, he was shocked. It was beautiful—just the right amount of masculine and feminine touches. "But some of this stuff is handmade. Who did that?" Nate asked. The doctor proudly said, "I did." He said he went to the craft store and found out how to make the things he wanted and just made them himself. Perhaps his Helpful People and Relationship corners were already working well for him, because he had no trouble acquiring help from the gals at the craft store.

Dumb and Dumber

Don't you just hate it when you can't make up your mind about something? Wouldn't it be great if you could ask someone else to choose what is best for you when you are stuck in the middle of a big decision? Well, if you have that magic eight ball working overtime, you may want to try this new approach with a friend. The fun thing about it is, you can get your friend to make up your mind without them even knowing the question. This technique uses visualization. This visualization uses the same universal wisdom and energy that feng shui uses. And the more you strengthen your visualization skills, the faster the feng shui will be able to change your life. So if you have enhanced the Skills and Knowledge area, but still find yourself in a quandary and feel you have to decide on something immediately, try this:

1. Write down three possible outcomes or choices and assign them a number. For example, if you are thinking about refinancing your house, you could write: "(1) Get a loan with a new bank. (2) Get a new loan with current bank. (3) Do not refinance at this time."
2. Tell a friend that you would like to take him on a guided visualization to help you with a decision.
3. Here's the fun part. You can take him anywhere. Pick something that you think would appeal to him or something that you think he could visualize well. Some of my favorites are the beach (three things wash up on shore), the mall (three new stores), the *Let's Make a Deal* show

(choose the box, the door, or the curtain), a new house (enter three rooms), and a restaurant (taste three dishes).

4. Tell him to close his eyes, and then describe where you are taking him. For example, you say: "There's a new mall in town. You decide to go. You enter and start to explore the interior. You are intrigued by what you see and become curious about some of the new stores. You come upon the first store and go in. Tell me about it." Then you let him tell you what he found inside—for example: "It's a Western wear store. There's some pretty neat stuff, but I don't wear this kind of stuff. I'm kind of bored and uninterested." Then you guide him up to the next store and let him describe what it is all about. He replies: "It's a great little gift shop, complete with fragrant candles, fun stationery, and cool T-shirts." You might ask him if he is interested in anything, to get him to describe how he feels about the store. Then he says, "Yea, this stuff is really cool. I would definitely come back to this store." Then it's off to the third store. He says, "Ugh. It's a hardware store. Icky fluorescent lights and obnoxious beeping forklifts. I'm aggravated. I wouldn't want to shop here." As he is describing the stores, you listen to his descriptions as if you asked him what he thought about refinancing. The western wear store (1) was the choice to get a loan from a new bank. The gift shop (2) was the choice to get a loan with your existing bank. And the hardware store (3) was the choice not to refinance at this time.

5. Finally, you lead him out of the place and ask something like, "Which store do you need to go back to, or would you like to go back to?" (Don't assume, by his descriptions, which one you think he would choose—it may surprise you.) He says, "I would go back to the Western wear store. Even though I don't use this stuff, I would go back to buy something for my dad for his birthday. It's my most immediate need right now."

6. From his reply, you should get a loan with a new bank—number one on your list. Even though he liked the stuff in the gift store (number two), he chose to go back to choice number one. He has made your decision about refinancing without even knowing it.

Everyone Is the Teacher and the Student

Relationships are the best classroom for gathering so many skills. Life's biggest lessons usually involve a relationship of some sort. Think back on what you learned so far about being a child, a peer, a best friend, an employee, a student while in a relationship with a parent or guardian, a peer, a friend, a boss, a teacher, and you'll see where I'm going here. It is no coincidence that Skills and Knowledge and Relationships and Love are directly opposite each other on the bagua (see Figure 39). Pick a cure and go for it. You won't regret it!

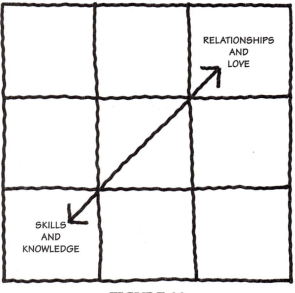

FIGURE 39

It's All in the Hands

Hands are the thing with this gua, so give those old callused, dry, or overworked paws a break and enhance this area for them.

Lucky Number 7

The vibration of the number 7 is the closest fit to the gua of Skills and Knowledge (wisdom). This number carries with it the energies of contemplation, inner strength, and spiritual enlightenment. If you find there are a lot of sevens in your life, you have hit the jackpot in the casino of wisdom. Watch out, though; if it's money you are after, your luck may have just run out—spiritual enlightenment and contemplation usually don't pay well in the material-wealth department.

Immediate Action Items for Skills and Knowledge

1. Get drugs, alcohol, and anything you smoke away from here.
2. Clear the clutter.
3. Add enhancements as necessary.

Skills and Knowledge in Summary

Power Tools: blue, books, light, food, things that remind you of wisdom, symbols of mentors or wise people, metal, water, black, wood, green, meditation items, altars of thanksgiving, symbols of the skills and knowledge you want to have.

Hazardous Materials: clutter, things that stop the thought process, unwise symbols.

Opposite Gua: Relationships and Love

Body Part: hand

Associated Number: 7

chapter 9

How Not to Play Family Feud—Family

O
h, that touchy subject—family. Everybody's got their own thoughts and feelings when they hear that word. To some, it brings back painful memories of sibling rivalry and teenage angst, and to others it's a feeling of belonging that cannot be re-created with anyone else. And there is every other possible thought and feeling in between. The Family area of the home is your foundation—your place of refuge and safety. If you don't have this, your world is endlessly affected. You may make decisions that come from fear instead of love—which will veer you from the happiness you should have in life. Family can be either blood relatives or not, so don't give up on this chapter if you have no blood relations.

If you intentionally move the appropriate feng shui stuff in the Family section of the home, you may

- ◉ feel more secure in all areas of your life
- ◉ improve your sex life
- ◉ build a stronger foundation that allows you to meet life's challenges with more confidence and less stress
- ◉ improve family relationships and bring harmony into family matters

- start being treated like one of the family by non–blood relatives
- enhance your business and increase your income
- get a promotion
- create a situation where you always have the money to cover the bills
- find balance with your emotional stability
- improve your physical and mental health
- make better choices in life

If you enter from the main door and head left toward the center of the wall on that side, you will find the Family area of the home (see Figure 40). The energy in this zone of the house influences how safe and secure you feel in life and how you relate to family members (blood relatives or not). The energy here

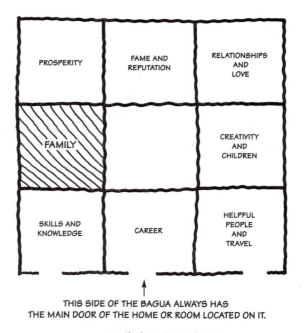

THIS SIDE OF THE BAGUA ALWAYS HAS
THE MAIN DOOR OF THE HOME OR ROOM LOCATED ON IT.

Family location in bagua.

FIGURE 40

is your foundation in life. Look around to see if you have been undermined in this area by the bad feng shui in your home.

Here are the power tools and hazardous materials you need to know about.

Power Tools for Family

Wood   Wood is the element for this area of the bagua. Wooden frames with family members in them are great in this area. If you have none, no big deal. There is plenty of other wooden stuff in the world. Sports fans, use your Louisville Slugger or hockey stick.

No wood around? Scrounge through kitchen drawers for toothpicks or chopsticks—a little wood is better than no wood.

Recycle the outdoors—gather up a bowl full of pine cones or acorns from under a tree and bring them in as symbolic seeds for family (watch out with the nuts if you already have a family full of them). Other wooden products are paper, wicker, rattan, and bamboo.

Green Stuff   Wood and green mean the same in feng shui, so if those family photos are in green wooden frames, so much the better. I asked a client of mine who said she wanted children to place a symbol of wood in this area of her home. I suggested a treelike plant. When I returned a few weeks later I saw that she had chosen a big branch of dead corkscrew willow that florists use in arrangements. What a choice for starting a new family! Moral of the story—no dead stuff.

No green, and you're desperate? Dig out that cheesy Saint Patrick's Day pub T-shirt you won last year in that drinking contest and put it to work here. If all else fails, try a wooden bowl full of avocados or artichokes. In the Family section, make your produce work for you.

Plants   Nurture them here and they will return the favor.

Rectangular or Columnar Objects   A vertically oriented rectangle symbolizes wood. Objects that have this shape can help bring in the ch'i you are looking for in this gua. About those green wooden frames we've been using—make them rectangular frames.

Water   We're back to the Creative Cycle again—water feeds wood. I enlarged three vacation pictures of Venice canals, complete with gondolas and striped poles, and placed them in the Family area of my master bedroom (which is in the Children gua of my home). They hang just above my black-framed *water* bed. Now, that's a lot of water—literal and symbolic. But the room is balanced with soft earth-toned walls and floral fabrics. My romantic Venice retreat did wonders for my family life—I have my new little son to prove it!

(My enlarged pictures are mounted on lightweight board and have no glass in front. I say this because hanging items over the head of a bed is sometimes unsettling—especially for those in earthquake-prone areas. Don't use this cure if you feel uneasy about anything overhead while you sleep.)

Black   Black is the water color. Use it here and see how things start to flow with family, children, and basic money needs.

Undulating Forms   Since water is the element that takes any shape, any shape other than round or triangular is considered OK here.

Hazardous Materials for Family

Metal   Sometimes my friends ask for my advice but don't really want to hear it. When she was visiting me, my friend Melody asked what feng shui tips I had for her home in Florida. (She was the one throwing all her pink stuff out in the Relationship chapter.) She said she found a cool metal bed and was going to buy it as soon as she got back home. I immediately explained to her that she would be placing this bed in her Family section of the home (Fame area of the room) and that it might get her out of balance with Family matters (metal chops wood). The news seemed to deflate her. Seeing that she really wanted to buy that bed, I then told her what I would do for someone who already had this problem. Red, the symbol for fire, would help to melt some of the metal; she could use the Destructive Cycle to her benefit in this fashion. (Red would also boost the Fame area of the room.) Since she didn't think red sheets or pillows or a red comforter were her thing (talk about making a red-hot love life!) I told her to tie red ribbons around the legs of the bed, and perhaps place some red cloth or felt under the mattress with the intention of reducing the impact of the metal. I also told her to get some water element item in the area. (Even though this is the Fame area of the room and water would seem to be destructive, the larger of the baguas—the Family gua of the home—needs to be in balance to support the room.) The water will create wood for her.

> Just as the universe holds our little tiny planet up in space, the planet holds the oceans and landmasses together. And just as those landmasses (let's say the environment or property) support our homes, the home supports the rooms within. And as the rooms hold the furnishings in order, the furnishings support the people who live with and use the furnishings. Good feng shui is always making sure the bigger picture is in balance so the smaller pictures can do their job.

I told her about all the power tools and hazardous materials for this space and let her make her mind up about what to do. She said she would reconsider the bed purchase, thanked me for the advice, and went back to Florida.

About three months later I get a call from her. "My family is driving me crazy! I'm about ready to disown all of them," she griped. I've know Melody for sixteen years and have never heard her talk about her family with such disgust. She was really peeved. After listening for a while I suddenly remembered our last visit and cut her off in midsentence, asking, "Did you buy that metal bed?" After a few silent seconds she replied, "Yea, but I put a two-by-four under it!"

"Did I say anything about a two-by-four? I don't think so!" I shrieked. "But if you really want a two-by-four in your house, I guess I can work with that. Obviously, the wood is still being overpowered by the metal. Either add more two-by-fours and pump up the feng shui with a bunch of intention, or get something red in there to take care of all that metal!"

What's a friend to do . . .

She has since added red candles, a red heart, and a red piece of flannel fabric to calm the metal, and (you guessed it) things have calmed down with the family as well.

White Stuff   White is the metal color and is not the best thing to have in the wood area. But if you do, here is an example with some helpful tips.

I happen to have a big white couch along the Family wall of my living room (the Health gua of the house). When I ordered the couch, I knew I would have to do something to balance it. But, of course, I didn't do it right away. I was pregnant (thanks to all the water in the master bedroom—oh yea, and my husband!) and I was trying to get the house done before the baby arrived. People were giving us all kinds of stuff for the baby, which was adding up to quite a pile in the storage room (Family gua of the house). I had my Prosperity corner of the storage room energized with all the goodies and could see the events unfolding that would bring me my fortunes, so I was not overly concerned with money. And since I was five months pregnant, I thought my family life looked great despite the baby clutter gaining strength in the storage room.

If you feel you have to have a gun in the house, for God's sake, do not place it in the Family section of anything. This is what I call *deadly metal*—not a good thing for Family.

Now, as I stated above, the Family part of the home is associated with money for the basics in life and is linked to the opposite gua—Children. Two months later I started to live the life of a person whose living room (in the center, or Health area, of the home) and storage room (Family) are out of balance.

My son was born—two months premature. He had to spend almost a month in the hospital—which, by the way, racked up a ton of bills. We used the money we had stashed away for quarterly taxes to pay the hospital and doctors. That also meant two months of lost working time, which made us cash poor in a hurry. Once the little guy got out of the hospital, we started accruing all the usual new baby bills and felt even more strapped. The one thing I did do when we finally brought him home from the hospital was totally feng shui his room—colored paper baguas everywhere (no time to paint)—and it seemed to work. He never ever got sick.

One day, I finally had time to get a hold of myself and take a look around to see what I could do. Then I remembered. I had never done anything with the white couch (my intention had been to buy a big throw in red tones to place on it). I quickly started cutting red triangles, black baguas, and green rectangles out of construction paper and taped them on the wall behind the couch. I kept adding them until I felt that there was enough of each (red to melt the metal, green for wood, and black for water to feed the wood).

Then I tore into the storage room, in the Family gua (now stuffed with baby junk). I organized, cleaned, and purged unnecessary items, and hung a crystal in the windowless room to brighten it up. I then reinforced it with intention and blessings (described in Chapter 12) and faithfully expected that every-

---

Construction paper makes a good cure because it's cheap and fast, and you can easily hide it.

thing would be all right ("faithfully expecting" is the toughest part of feng shui when you are in the middle of a crisis).

And here is the result of doing all that.

In less than one month, my husband's grandmother offered to pay off the rest of the hospital bills. Two months later, out of the clear blue, my mother gave us several thousand dollars, which got Uncle Sam off our backs. And about a week after that, my husband's mother told us that she would be managing and paying all of the family's health insurance premiums. I don't know about you, but I have never had someone offer to pay any of my bills in my life. All the results came through *family* members and had to do with *health* and *children*—the three areas affected by my feng shui intentions.

When Cole was about fourteen months, I finally committed to creating a real baby room for him and losing the temporary feng shui look (all those paper baguas taped around the room were getting pretty droopy). I took everything down to paint the walls. Would you believe, within forty-eight hours he had his first ear infection? Upon returning from the doctor, I immediately threw up a bagua daisy and hung a crystal from the center of the room's ceiling. Cole was back to himself within two days, without antibiotics.

Even though I am a feng shui consultant, sometimes I can also get caught up in the moment and feel as if there's no connection between my stuff and my life. But after these kinds of events, I become more of a believer than ever. I also think I am a better feng shui consultant because of it.

Round Things   This is not the best place for the set of white china, the heirloom doilies, or the coveted baseball collection, because round is the symbolic shape for metal.

"Charlie Brown" Trees   I visited a home where there stood, in the heart of the Family section, the saddest little excuse for a plastic fig tree I have ever seen. This thing was limp, dusty, and leaning out of the pot at about sixty degrees. I said to the owner, "Well, here is your family tree. What do you think?"

"*Yikes!* I get it!" she said as she tossed the little tree out of the house.

(Change this hazardous material to a power tool for Family by replacing it with a beautiful, healthy, strong tree—a tree that represents what you are looking for in your family. I would also give it a name, and lovingly treat it like a family member.)

A Family Only Jerry Springer Could Love

There's one in every family—the black sheep, the oddball, the total embarrassment—the family member that thrives on stirring up the rest of the family. Let's say for now it's Uncle Ned. He is driving you nuts. His idea of fun is tormenting everyone with his sick humor and sarcastic snotty comebacks to everything said. Your personal opinion of him is that he single-handedly robs you of any real quality of life. You definitely don't have loving thoughts of him often. The thought of applying feng shui to your Family area appeals to you, but then you fear you may accidentally bump Ned off because of your less than pure thoughts of him. Although life with Ned sucks, you don't need the guilt trip.

Don't worry. If your intentions are in the right place, you cannot hurt anyone. The universe understands intentions and doesn't make mistakes. Enhancing the feng shui energies in the Family gua can make one of the following three things happen in an Uncle Ned situation:

1. The person with whom you are out of harmony suddenly or slowly changes, and eventually stops bugging you. (Ned shuts up.)
2. You change. (Ned keeps dishing out his weird antics, but miraculously, he no longer gets under your skin.)
3. The situation of imbalance is removed from your life for as long as needed. (Ned suddenly decides to take a trip around the world for a year.)

If you intend to find better balance in your family and you leave the specific outcome up to the universe, the situation will resolve itself in the best way possible.

Family Ties

Family members possess some of the strongest loyalty possible. Loyalty binds very tightly. The Family gua is associated with the virtue of loyalty. Whether you seek loyalty from your parents, coworkers, roommates, or friends, loyal people are awesome to have around. It's just nice sometimes to have someone else go to bat for you for a change. The mafia and the Kennedy family are two great examples of such family loyalty. You know you're in a sacred circle if you are a member of either one of these clans. Having roots in loyal ancestry can be very beneficial throughout life. Strong roots stabilize your foundation. Strong roots help the family tree grow. Roots, trees—is it any wonder that wood is the element for this gua?

Family Heirlooms

Sometimes inheriting or receiving stuff is not all that it's cracked up to be. Let's talk about the physical stuff first. I don't care how much money it is worth, or how long it has been in the family; if you've been given something that you either don't love or can't use, it's dragging you down. This type of clutter (the type that has either a sentimental memory or a guilt trip attached to it) is so hard to give up, but giving it up is necessary for you to remain steadfast in your intention to stay clear about family issues. Try to find a new home for the possessions (a museum, a charity, another family member, a friend). When my grandfather died, my mother asked if there was anything I wanted from his house. I replied, "A flour sifter." It was all I could think of that I needed at the time, and I had specific fond memories of baking with my long-since-deceased grandmother. Anything else (except cash) would have been clutter for me.

And if you receive a gift that you don't like or can't use, don't buy into the guilt of having to display it in your home. Consider it an energy sucker. Don't keep guilt trips around— who needs 'em? Not you! I remember specifically saying to my mother right before she and Dad were going off to vacation in Germany, "Whatever you do, don't bring me back a Hummel." Dusting little German porcelain figures on shelves is not my idea of a good time—I don't care how much the little buggers appreciate in value.

Use it or lose it.

Now it's time to bring up the nonphysical stuff that gets passed down the lineage—stuff like a sense of lack, or a sense of shame, or buying into a disease that "runs in the family." Because they are invisible, inheritances like these are harder to detect, but they are as debilitating as the physical clutter. Many people who have grown up in hard times pass on the legacy that the world is a hard place to live or that you have to work real hard just to get by. Some do this subconsciously; others spread these tales "for your own good." Spending the time to sift through the mental clutter you have been handed is probably one of the most cathartic processes you could do in your life. A great way to start the process is to enhance your Family gua (for ancestry), the Skills and Knowledge area (for the wisdom to know what to do), and the Fame gua (for the courage to press forward in tough conditions). Piggybacking this with professional help might also be a good idea if you've been dealt a big hand.

Just because someone is dishing it out doesn't mean you have to take it.

The Choice Is Yours—Make It a Good One

If you have your Skills and Knowledge area cranked up and still find yourself making poor choices, enhance the Family gua of the home. Being taken care of is what this gua is all about. If you are taken care of, you come from a more powerful place in life, and are thereby able to make clearer decisions. On the other hand, if you are worrying about paying rent and feel as if you are drifting and have no stable foundation in life, your decision making will reflect that.

Claire was unemployed for a number of months. She got so freaked out by it, she started thinking about every dime she spent. Instead of making calls to get work, she started to just read the paper and mail résumés. Instead of going to the monthly network lunch, she ate lunch at home alone. Instead of buying the power suit, she lived in her sweats, saving her nice clothes for when she got a job.

Claire is coming from a place of fear. She is missing opportunities, which only enhances her chances of remaining unemployed. Remember, when you enhance your home with feng shui, you place your order with the universe. You *must* believe the universe took your order and is working on it. By putting all her available energy into saving her money and sparing her clothes, Claire was giving those concerns the power, instead of empowering her feng shui order. *Energy follows thought.* Her energy was very busy conserving money, and not out job hunting.

Healing Old Wounds

If you have enhanced your home properly and waited with full faith, but find something is still missing in your life, come on back to the Family section. There may be stuck ch'i from a childhood trauma still affecting you (though you are not even aware of it). Sit quietly in this part of your home, meditate, or simply ask for healing. If you want to know what that something missing is all about, ask for it to be revealed to you. But I have found that knowing is not necessary to receive healing.

Here are two clearing rituals, the first for clearing the distant past, the second for more recent events:

1. Get three new pieces of red paper and a brand-new black-ink pen. Write all the things to be cleared on the red papers. If you think there is something in the past that you may have blocked out of your memory, write that it be released as well, even though your consciousness won't let you remember it. At noon or midnight, burn the papers and ask that these things be released from your energy. Give thanks.

2. Each night before you go to sleep, review your day for any events that happened that you view as negative. If there is something that either you wish didn't happen or wish you could change, play it again in your mind and mentally change the outcome to something positive. The quicker you change it, the less time it has to impact you energetically.

Stay in the present. Don't drag the energy from the past along with you any-more. Release it by forgiving.

| Claim Your Space |

Even though the little munchkins don't usually pay any rent, it is important that kids have a space of their own. Whether it be a whole room or a small area of a room that is theirs and theirs alone, it is important that each member of the home have a sense of space and boundaries.

If a family member appears to be ungrounded (showing signs of drifting apart or making bad decisions), place rounded rocks in each of the corners of the house or in each of the bagua areas. Rocks placed in the center of a room (perhaps under a bed) work as well.

A good feng shui practitioner always asks each child (or any tenant who did not specifically request the presence of the feng shui consultant) if it is OK to enter their room or space.

If you are living with someone who does not share your taste, you may be living with items in your home that you hate (that old sad clown painting that your in-laws gave you, or your roommate's bulldogs-playing-poker picture hung over the toilet). This may be draining you of much-needed positive energy. Review these items with all family members or roommates, discuss your feelings candidly, and see if it is OK that they be removed from the house. If others are too attached to them and want them to remain, try to designate a specific space where they can display the things they love—hopefully a space that you live in or walk by most infrequently.

Love it or lose it.

Hang Up Your Hang-Ups About Sex

If your parents ever sat you down for *the talk,* you know how awkward it can get when family members and the sex topic cross paths. But for better or worse, most of your ideas, thoughts, and hang-ups about sex came from the family you grew up with, whether the talk actually ever took place or not. When you think about it, you should probably cut your parents some slack. After all, they got most of their hang-ups from their parents. (Big tip—avoid mental pictures now.)

The people who raised you have either consciously or sub-consciously filled your mind with many values, including those regarding sex, just as their forebears filled theirs. Hang-ups could come from religious ideals, sociocultural ideas, or simply a bad translation of someone truly trying to pass down good information. So, if there is a hang-up in your sex life, a good place to start to repair or treat this problem is the Family area of the home. Because you were raised a particular way, with certain thoughts about sex ingrained deeply within you, it may be hard to review such information objectively. But if you do suspect you have been misinformed, place an item (go back to power tools) in the Family area with the specific intention of allowing yourself to distinguish between the truths and untruths you have been told about sex. Ask that you have the courage to change (enhance Fame and Reputation for this courage) so that you can live life fully, lovingly, and hang-up free. Here is a sample affirmation: "I live my life free from any untruths regarding sex. I fully forgive anyone who has misinformed me."

Ward, I'm Worried About the Beaver

Since the Children and Family guas are directly opposite, they affect each other greatly. If you have specific challenges with your children and you've got every power tool imaginable in the Children and Creativity area, try adding to the Family zone. A traditional cure for increasing family strength and getting children connected back in with the family is to buy a new plant for each child and one plant for the parents together. Place these plants in the Family area of the master bedroom. Tie one red ribbon around all the plants and sleep nine nights with them that way. After that time, take nine pinches of dirt from the plant representing the parents and place them in each of the kids' plants. Then place each child's plant in the Children section of their room or space. This is one of those traditional cures that is very symbolic and ritualistic but is found to work quite well.

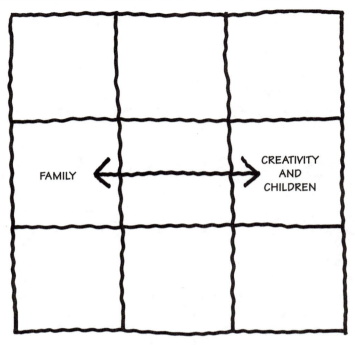

FIGURE 41

Also, since the Family gua is about solid foundation and the Creativity and Children gua is about freedom, add to your Creativity if you feel too set in your ways.

Happy Feet

Since the foot is the body part associated with the Family section of the home, it would be wise to enhance this area if there are any health concerns related to either of those little doggies. Ladies, still stuffing your toes into pointy pumps? ("Ouch!"— for fashion as well as health.) Give them a breather by massaging this area.

The Four Corners of the Earth

The number that best describes the Family gua is 4. Four is stable and secure, whole and united—as a family should be.

Immediate Action Items for Family

1. Remove all guns from this area.
2. Mend or repair anything that needs it.
3. Add enhancements as necessary.

| Family in Summary |

Power Tools: wood, green, plants, rectangular or columnar objects, water, black, undulating forms.

Hazardous Materials: metal, white, round stuff, "Charlie Brown" trees.

Opposite Gua: Children and Creativity

Body Part: foot

Associated Number: 4

chapter 10

Just for the Health of It—Health

ive the center, or Health area, of your home a feng shui workout and you'll see

- ⊙ more optimal health
- ⊙ a sense of balance in life
- ⊙ betterment in life situations that you couldn't fit into any other area of the home's bagua

I use this area of the home to enhance health concerns because it is the epitome of balance—complete yin and yang energies. If your physical body is in balance, you can go about achieving everything you set out to do, giving it your all. I have heard this area of the home described as the place where everything *and* nothing happens.

The only way feng shui could possibly not work is if you (that is, your physical, mental, and spiritual energies) are so out of whack you override its forces by draining the energy away from it. If you get no results from feng shui, the only space left to look at that may be affecting the outcome is inside yourself. The Health part of the home deals with just that. And by the

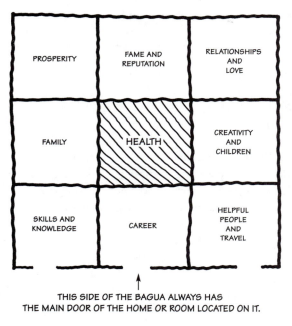

THIS SIDE OF THE BAGUA ALWAYS HAS
THE MAIN DOOR OF THE HOME OR ROOM LOCATED ON IT.

Health location in bagua.
FIGURE 42

way, unless you are a Helen Keller or a Christopher Reeve, whose physical challenges are an inspiration to many and appear to be an integral aspect of their life path, there is no reason to have anything less than optimal health.

Where is the center, and do I have to measure to find it? No measuring necessary. All of the bagua areas subtly blend into one another just like the colors of the rainbow. There's no need for exact measurements anywhere. (See Figure 42.) And the center of the bagua is even less exact than the other guas. It reaches out and touches each of the other eight areas of the home. So declare that *your* center, or Health gua, is somewhere in or near the middle of the home and decorate it accordingly. Choose a table against a wall to display your feng shui symbols if there is nothing but thin air in the exact center. It will be close enough to this gua to cause the ch'i to change. The only place not recommended for placing your health accoutrements is near the Career area of a home or room, because earth dams water.

Here are the best and worst things for health in feng shui—speak.

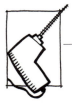

Power Tools for Health

Earth   Earth is the element for the center. The element can be introduced to a space quite simply by adding a healthy plant in a pot made of earth material and color. As long as it is not a tree (remember, wood uproots earth) almost any plant will do. Try to choose a plant that says "healthy and happy" to you. If you must use a silk plant because of light restrictions, place nine tablespoons of real soil into the pot to make it "real" in a feng shui way.

By the way, for all you slobs out there trying to take a short-cut, dirty stuff does not count as an earth element.

Things Made of Earth   There are many beautiful items made from earthen materials that can be intentionally placed for health and balance. China and ceramics, clay tiles, clay pots, brick, and natural stone flooring can make beautiful reminders of health. The flooring in my home is square and bagua-shaped terra-cotta tiles—how perfect is that?

Fruit   A bowl of fresh fruit can do wonders for your health whether you eat it or not. It symbolizes many things—good luck, prosperity, hospitality, and health. So place it in the center space of your home and invite health into your life.

Funny Stuff   Laughter is a great cure for health, so place anything that cracks you up here. Laughter is truly the best medicine. Videos of funny movies, comedy acts, or bloopers; photos of yourself or friends taken in fun moments; those too-good-to-throw-away greeting cards; gag gifts—all work here. Even if it's not a total knee-slapper, if it brings a smile to your face, it fits. Simple things like a hummingbird ornament, a child's picture, or an old love letter are just a few items in this little-smile category.

> Giving someone a reason to laugh is one of the greatest gifts you can give. And the strange thing is, it's usually free and priceless at the same time.

Yellow, Gold, and Other Earth Tones   The colors of earth are the colors for this space. The banana in the fruit bowl and the dirt in the plant pot can do the trick for keeping you healthy. I take yellow flowers to my friends when they need a little umph in the health department.

Squares   The square is the shape for this area. Square-tile floors, square tables, and square dancing are all effective in this area. (Actually, I just made up the part about square dancing, but I don't think it would hurt!)

Symbols of Earth   Pictures of mountains or farmland both work. A globe does too. I like to use natural stones or crystals. They make me feel grounded and in touch with Mother Earth.

Horizontal or Flat Things   A square stone tabletop in this area is a great replica of earth in feng shui terms. I have my square flat wedding album on my square stone coffee table in the living room next to a plant and three rust-colored candles.

Although you can't get much flatter than pancakes and pizzas (I hear my brutally honest dear friends in my inner ear now saying, "No Karen, you're wrong—your chest is much flatter!"), they're just too temporary to be considered.

Fire   The element of fire makes earth in the Creative Cycle, so use it to your advantage here. A little candle can do a big job in this part of the house. If your fireplace is in the middle of the house, you are practically home free. Just make sure it is in good working order.

Stars and Sun   These are elements of fire that especially work well in this area. They can be symbolized by items for sun such as sunflowers, sundials, and pictures of sunrises or sunsets, and by starfish, the Stars and Stripes, or the Star of David for stars. A copy of the video *A Star Is Born* is questionable but probably has merit.

Religious Objects   And speaking of the Star of David, any religious object you connect with works very well here.

Red   You got it. If fire is good, then red is too. Red candles, place mats, or runners can help that table I spoke of. A red-tasseled lamp shade works. A nice throw on the couch does too. Red functions great for Health. Every year a friend of mine places a big bowl of red Christmas ornaments on her living room table. Until I learned feng shui, I never knew why that made me feel so good when I saw it. Besides invigorating the ch'i by holiday decorating, the red gave the room the warmth and balance it struggled for during the rest of the year.

Triangular or Pyramid-Shaped Objects   The symbolic shape of fire can heat up the health spot of the home.

Hazardous Materials for Health

Wood   Wood is the destructive force that uproots earth, robbing it of its nutrients and water. So, in the earth area of the home, it is not wise to have wooden stuff, especially in the form of trees or treelike plants. Even that big fake ficus plant had better move out into another area (preferably the Family or Fame area) because it symbolizes a tree. But as I said before, if you have to have it here, do something to balance it. Place it in a big white pot (white symbolizes metal) or at least place white, red, and yellow paper in or under the pot to add the fire and earth. (If you aren't getting this Creative and Destructive Cycle stuff by now, go back and review Chapter I.)

Green   Since green means wood—you guessed it—no green. The green leaves of nontreelike plants are the exception to this rule, so small plants can stay.

Columnar or Rectangular Objects   Like the towering trees of wood, tall columns and other tall, rectangular objects don't belong here. If you're stuck with this situation, mitigate it by using the Destructive Cycle for wood (white, round, and so on) and enhance the earth element for greater strength.

Spiral Staircases   Stairways in general are a scary subject in any area, but a spiral staircase can be a feng shui nightmare. First of all, spiral staircases usually don't have risers, which really ticks off the ch'i (it keeps falling through). Second, with the spiraling pattern, the ch'i gets so dizzy and disoriented that by the time it gets to the bottom, it's a dysfunctional mess. And finally, these staircases are usually made of metal or wood, which may conflict with the section of the home they are located in. For example, if you have a wooden spiral staircase in the middle of your home, it would be very wise to counteract it so your health does not suffer.

Anywhere you have a spiral staircase, take special precautions to alleviate the ch'i from corkscrewing into the ground and out of your life. Here are some ways to do that:

1. Remove the staircase or replace it. It sounds expensive and probably is. Don't worry, here are more alternatives . . .

2. Take a piece of fabric or a strand of silk greenery and wrap it around the metal center post of the staircase from top to bottom (remember, as long as it doesn't look like a tree, green is OK). You can also wrap the banister. If you can, grow a real vine on it! Weird, but it can be effective. And if all of this is too tacky for you . . .

3. Paint the staircase (or at least the underside of the treads) the color of the area of the bagua you are in. You can also use the Creative or Destructive Cycle colors to your benefit—a white metal spiral staircase in the Family area could be painted red (to melt it), or black (to feed wood), or green (to simply add more wood). And if painting is out of the picture . . .

4. Light the staircase from above to lift the ch'i, or hide mirrors under the stairs facing up to reflect the ch'i back up.

Desperate Times Call for Desperate Measures

As a feng shui consultant, I find that I am often called in after everything else has not worked. When the situation gets to a point of desperation and there's nothing left to lose—well, let's give ol' feng shui a try. That's OK, and I can work with that, but geez, why go through the crappy stuff if you don't have to?

Dear friends of mine were in this position. They had recently moved into a beautiful, brand-new home in southern California. Don and Laura were both in high-paying sales positions, which allowed them to decorate their home meticulously and beautifully. Unfortunately for Don, his new position in bed was not as meticulously thought out as the home decor. (See Figure 43.) A bathroom door aligned with the foot of the bed. The double-door entry into the bedroom also aligned with the bottom of the bed on his side, at a forty-five degree angle. Right outside the double doorway into the bedroom was a huge sweeping spiral staircase—right in the middle of the house, the Health area and center of the home. And the real topper: a huge silk ficus tree graced the center of the sweeping staircase.

In less than six months of living there, Don was stricken with an illness that affected his legs, making it too painful to walk. The doctors to this day still aren't completely sure what it was. He was hospitalized for over two weeks, where he submitted to every test imaginable.

The day he was admitted, Laura asked me to come over and see what I could do. I immediately hung a crystal between the bathroom door and the bottom of the bed (with the intention of dispersing the ch'i). I laid down a red line of tape across the bedroom door frame (with the intention of stopping the ch'i from flowing out the door and down the staircase). And I placed mirrors in the closet under the staircase, facing up (with the in-

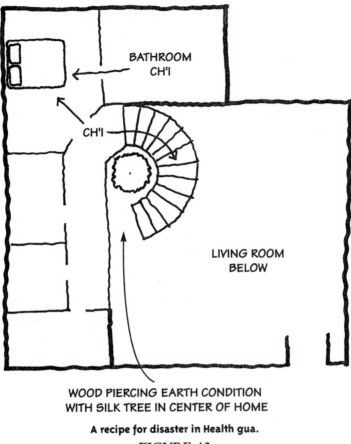

**WOOD PIERCING EARTH CONDITION
WITH SILK TREE IN CENTER OF HOME**

A recipe for disaster in Health gua.

FIGURE 43

tention of keeping the ch'i lifted). I also did a visualization that the staircase had bunches of helium-filled balloons tied to the railing (to keep things "looking up").

Then we talked about the tree. This thing was so big there really was no other place to put it. I suggested removing it, but I could tell Laura was hesitant. So, I did the next best thing. I placed white and yellow all around the pot between the basket and the pot, and added real earth to the pot (with intention, of course).

I gave her cures "to go"——to take to the hospital in case there were major faux pas in his room (trust me, there usually are). Then, I rang my Tibetan bell for clearing negative energies and sent them on their way. (See more on space clearing in Chapter 11.)

As mysteriously as Don got sick, he gradually turned around, and today is running at 100 percent. The only thing the doctors did was give him huge amounts of antibiotics for several weeks in case he had some kind of infection; and once he started to get better, they pronounced that he indeed must have had one.

I know some of you are wondering about the cures to go. I find it very common to see feng shui messes in places like hotels and hospitals. I gave Laura some red tape, to stop any ch'i in line with Don's bed (such as from the bathroom door); a crystal, in case there was any arrow ch'i (remember, no angles pointing toward the bed); and some red ribbon, to tie around the legs of the bed if it was metal and in the Family section of the room. And finally, I gave her a bag of salt (you can use rock salt, kosher, Epsom, or sea salt) so she could place some in a bowl of water under his bed, to absorb any negative energy (think of how many sick people have been in that bed before he got there).

If I Had Only Known Then What I Know Now . . .

It is always so easy to look back and trace the trail to demise. Now I use feng shui to ward it off before it happens. The following story is a little depressing, but it had so many good feng shui lessons, I am compelled to include it despite its seriousness.

I will use my friend Gary as an example to show how a living space perpetuated mental illness. Gary was a very successful businessman bachelor who truly appreciated the finest money could buy—food, decor, furniture, cars, and the rest. He was meticulous about his seaside apartment, having a housekeeper vacuum every day and care for the large indoor plants. He was very generous with his time, money, material possessions. He was an excellent cook who prided himself on knowing the latest recipes and having the latest cooking utensils. He loved to eat. Under the advice of a doctor, he went on a supervised liquid diet to counter his ever-increasing obesity after a debilitating back injury. He decided that since he had previously quit smoking cold turkey, he could do this diet. So he cleaned out every item of food in the house and began. (Symbolically, he removed his prosperity, his love, *and* his physical sustenance.) He thought he could ignore the natural feelings of lack and vulnerability that came from being on such a diet. He simply turned his back on his love of fine food and social outings.

He was on the liquid diet for about five months. He lost a lot of weight but was never the same. Although I believe his illness was a lifetime struggle just waiting to resurface, it seemed this diet was the catalyst that sent him back into its depths again. He started becoming paranoid, which caused him to fire his housekeeper. The apartment started to get quite messy, and all the plants died (accumulating clutter and dead ch'i). He then began to suffer serious symptoms of clinical depression—one symptom being the total inability to do anything, even get out of bed, talk on the phone, or leave the house (*very* stuck ch'i). His business dried up. He began drinking (bad for wisdom). Despite his son's and two friend's efforts to find help, he vehemently refused it. He started selling art off the walls to pay rent. The paranoia worsened to a point where he tacked black plastic over the windows (really bad for positive ch'i flow). Since he couldn't leave, he had to rely on friends to deliver food and sundries. Money started quickly disappearing (like people, money doesn't like to stick around depressing situations). He sold his truck, Jaguar, and business equipment for next to nothing because his paranoid fear of confrontation left him with the inability to negotiate. Clothes started piling up, along with empty two-liter soda bottles and garbage (more ch'i-stagnating clutter). One day when I visited, he said he couldn't believe how his microwave and regular oven, two VCRs, and one television had all broken down within a week (direct result of stuck ch'i). Money was now very scarce, and after thirteen years of living in the once beautiful apartment, he was evicted. The final picture in my mind of this situation was this: dead plants lying on the floor, now covered with at least an inch of dust, a stench from dirty sheets and clothes, piles of mail by the door, including legal notices, and a curled-up Gary in bed. We finally called the county mental health department for intervention.

Although this event occurred before I was taught feng shui, I look back with my feng shui eyes now and see the negative spiral he was in with his environment. The simple event of denying himself food and removing it from the house started him on a path that resulted in a total loss of everything—health, prosperity, reputation, relationships, career, family, helpful people, children, and wisdom. Such a simple, seemingly harmless change of environment caused a catastrophic chain of events. I often wonder how things would have been different if he hadn't thrown out all of his basic-sustenance ch'i by removing all food.

Feng Shui, the Real Maytag Repairman

You might be wondering what the deal was with all Gary's appliances breaking down at the same time. I think it was no coincidence. If the center of your home is healthy, your stereo, fax, car, computer, and appliances will be too. Give these items names and treat them like friends. I know, I know, it sounds weird, but is it the first thing that sounds weird in this book?

The Weight of the World Is on My Shoulders, Thighs, Hips, and Abdomen

I personally feel that if you properly apply feng shui to all the areas of your home, you won't have a weight problem. But for those of you out there who think that's a cop-out, here's my quick-fix cure for obesity: Place a mirror facing out toward you on the refrigerator. If your downfall is the cabinet that houses the megamorsel cookies and the deep-fried pork rinds, mirror it as well. Mirrored cabinetry—it could catch on. Who knows?

And if you consistently use a kitchen door to enter your home, either screen the kitchen from view somehow or (I may be getting too complicated here) *use another door!* If Cheez-Its and Funyuns are the first things you see each time you come home, you may be prone to heavy calorie pounding before you get a chance to think about what you're doing. One client of mine who had this situation installed a Japanese curtain in the doorway to the kitchen. It helped that she was of Japanese descent, but it may work for you too.

Room with a View
(For One Eyeball, Anyway)

The feng shui term *split view* refers to a situation in which, when you enter a room and look forward, one eye focuses on a close wall straight ahead and the other focuses on a wall, space, or object farther away (see Figure 44). This condition can cause im-

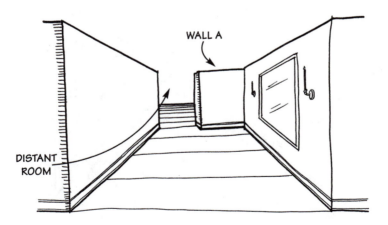

A split view is created by Wall A when you try to look into the distant room. The right eye focuses close on the wall and the left eye focuses at a distance.

FIGURE 44

balance and may show up several ways. It is a problem anywhere in the home—not just the Health gua.

A client recently had a split view upon entering his home. When I asked him if he had any feelings of instability, imbalance, or fatigue, he responded, "Well, I have just started seeing a psychologist because I think I have everything and should be happy, but deep down I'm not. Could that be it?" You see, split views make us see two things at the same time. In his case, it showed up as confusion about being happy and sad.

The cures for this are simple. Place in the space something stunning that completely catches your attention (with both eyes) upon entering, so you focus on it instead. This could be a beautiful flower arrangement, a piece of art, or a big colorful bird in a cage. You could actually place an outrageous object in front of the wall that creates the split view (see Figure 45). Another alternative is to mirror the closer wall to "make it disappear," thereby allowing your eyes to focus at a farther distance.

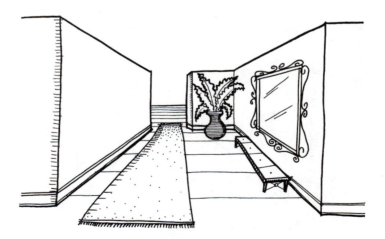

Add elements that command both eyes to look either on or in front of Wall A, or into the distant room, to cure a split view.

FIGURE 45

The Body Bases Are Covered

By now you know the other eight areas of the home and their associated body parts. But if you have an ailment other than the foot, hip, eye, mouth, head, ear, hand, or organs, don't worry. The center has got you covered. It takes care of any other body part *and* any other life situation you can think of that is not covered by the preceding eight guas. So enhance this area if you don't think your particular problem fits into any of the other guas. Isn't that tidy—an area of the home for anything else! As I said before, feng shui can benefit any condition.

Nine Ladies Dancing

Nine is the number most closely associated with this part of the home. The number 9 is the highest digit of the lineup, and also the highest in humanitarianism. If you live in a 9 house you will be prone to thinking high thoughts (like the big picture in life) and will be able to reach once-considered-unattainable heights. Since it is the last of the numbers in the lineup as well, 9 is prone to complete things and resolve old issues. Don't lose sight of yourself in the process, though—keep the balance and it will seem like an effortless dance.

Immediate Action Items for Health

1. Place metal (candlesticks, tray, and the like) on top of any wooden table that is in the middle of the room.
2. Cure spiraling staircases anywhere in the home.
3. Add enhancements as necessary.

| Health in Summary |

Power Tools: earth, items made from earth, fruit, funny stuff, yellow, gold, earth tones, squares, symbols of earth, horizontal or flat items, fire, stars and sun, religious objects, red, triangular or pointy objects.

Hazardous Materials: wood, green, columnar or rectangular objects, spiral staircases.

Opposite Gua: none

Body Part: all other body parts not specifically mentioned in other guas

Associated Number: 9

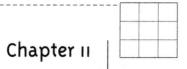

Chapter 11

*Our House Is a
Very, Very, Very Strange House*

This chapter will answer some of the questions about unique home configurations that might come up when using feng shui. After all, not everyone lives in a perfectly square or rectangular home. Different scenarios will be discussed that, with a little intuition and imagination, can fit a myriad of conditions.

Commonly Asked Questions and Cures

My home is not square. How does the bagua work then?

There are a few items to take into consideration when doing a basic feng shui makeover. Missing pieces are a crucial consideration. If you have one or more pieces missing when you overlay the bagua onto the home, you have a place in the home that is not supporting you. And if it is not supporting you, your own personal energy is used to make up the difference. You get drained and are left weak in the area of your life associated with the missing space.

In Figure 46, the Prosperity section of the home is missing. This may show up in your life as money going out as fast as it comes in, or perhaps as your need to work way too hard for

An L-shaped home.
FIGURE 46

every morsel of money you get. Part of the Children and Creativity gua is missing as well. In this situation, perhaps it's your kids who are draining your wallet.

But don't worry, there are several ways to correct this situation. Yes, you could hire a contractor to build an addition to your home that would fill in the missing piece, but that probably would incur great expense. If you don't want to call the contractors, try one of these methods.

For completing the corner using the space outdoors, carefully place vertical or horizontal objects exactly where the two walls would meet if the piece were not missing (see Figure 47). Or you can create "outdoor walls" with linear items. Several variations will work to complete a missing piece. Remember, using symbolism when making an adjustment like this adds strength. For example, if the Relationship corner is missing, one solution for the exact corner is a redbud tree. It has heart-shaped leaves. (Of course, you have to consider whether that tree grows in your climate or not.) Another example: If the Skills and Knowledge corner is missing, create an outdoor space with a statue of a sitting Buddha, Solomon, or another wise per-

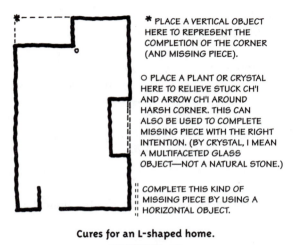

Cures for an L-shaped home.

FIGURE 47

son as a focal point. Pour a concrete patio and place pennies with wise ol' Lincoln on them into the concrete.

Below are a few other alternatives for fixing missing pieces by placing an element where the corner of the home should be.

Vertical Objects

- ⊙ tree
- ⊙ flagpole
- ⊙ light pole
- ⊙ maypole
- ⊙ tetherball pole
- ⊙ clothesline pole
- ⊙ outdoor fireplace with chimney (Watch the elements with this one. It's not the best for the Creativity section.)
- ⊙ fountain with water spray at corner (unless completing the Fame section)
- ⊙ gazebo or other outdoor architectural structure
- ⊙ trellis or fence
- ⊙ garden walls
- ⊙ hedge
- ⊙ sculpture or large pot

- ⊙ sundial
- ⊙ child's play structure

Flat or Horizontal Objects

- ⊙ a red line sprayed on paving where the walls should be (You can also bury red string or ribbon underground to complete the form.)
- ⊙ stones, bricks, or tiles lined up to complete the configuration
- ⊙ a pool or other water feature (best if rounded in form so no angles point at the home)
- ⊙ a crystal buried at the corner (either multifaceted glass or natural)
- ⊙ fire pit
- ⊙ sand box

For completing the corner using the indoor space (say, because there's a pool outside right where your completed corner would be), use the same cure as for arrow ch'i. Place a crystal inside the home at the corner that pokes into the house (again, see Figure 47). Intend that the crystal cure the missing piece. Also, remember to adjust the elements as well—for example, if the pool in the example above is in the Fame gua.

If you did your best with the exterior and interior cures and your life still feels a bit out of balance, here are two more suggestions. The first option is to give extra attention to the same gua that the home has missing in each room. Using Figure 46 as an example, make sure each room in the home has strong Prosperity and Creativity guas. The second option is to employ the cover-your-butt cure mentioned in the "Checks and Balances" section of Chapter 1 in the same places.

Parts of my home jut out toward the street and are in front of the front door. How does the bagua overlay in this situation? Is the "front door" out in the yard somewhere?

You will get different answers from different feng shui consultants on this one. My advice would be to start at the front door as usual and place the bagua over the parts of the home that fall behind it. Then take a look at which part of the home is in front of the front door and see if it is necessary to bring it "into" the home. If it is a junky garage, leave it out. If it is your child's bedroom, bring it in (see Figure 48).

Without proper adjustments, whatever space or room is poking out in front of the front door is outside the home's main energy pattern. If it is the kitchen, the inhabitants may never cook and may find themselves eating out a lot. Or worse yet, one spouse eats out a lot and leaves the other one home alone.

If it is a child's bedroom, the child may leave home at a young age. (This works both ways. If you have an adult "kid" that won't fly the coop and you have a bedroom in front of the

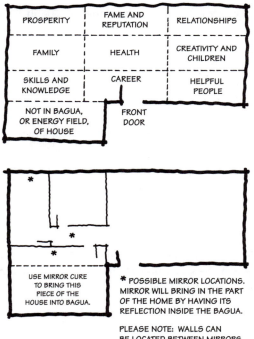

When part of your home is outside your home.

FIGURE 48

front door, move them there to symbolically place them outside of the house. Maybe they will get the hint and start packing.)

If you have an office in the home, this may be the room to use so it does not nag at you so much while you are at home.

Here are some of the best uses for space in front of the front door:

- in-laws' quarters
- adult "child"
- home office
- messy hobby or storage room
- garage
- bathroom

Here are uses that definitely should not be in front of the front door:

- master bedroom
- small child's room
- kitchen

If you have a room in front of the house's main door that needs to be brought in, simply place a mirror (preferably bagua shaped, but that's not necessary) anywhere inside the home facing the "outside" room. (There can be walls between the mirror and this room, as in Figure 48.) Give the mirror the job of bringing the room into the home with your intention.

A big chunk of my bagua falls in the apartment next door and I'm pretty sure the guy who lives there would think I'm crazy if I mentioned feng shui to him. How can I complete my missing piece?

This type of multitenant living can result in mixed energies with your neighbor if indeed his apartment completes yours. You'll find you have to use extra energy to overcome this situation without a feng shui cure. Place a plant, crystal, or chime at the corner of the two walls where the neighbor's apartment pokes into yours (see Figure 49). As well as curing the arrow ch'i, this can cure the missing part. Give it strong intention that it is being placed there to overcome this unsatisfactory ch'i condition.

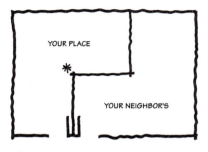

COMPLETE THE SHAPE
OF YOUR APARTMENT AND
STOP ARROW CH'I WITH A
✳ PLANT, CHIME, OR CRYSTAL.

When part of your home falls in someone else's home.

FIGURE 49

Does the shed built onto the side of the house count? (I can only get into it from the outside.)

Anything attached to the house that is under solid roof can affect the energy of a home (see Figure 50). Just as applying

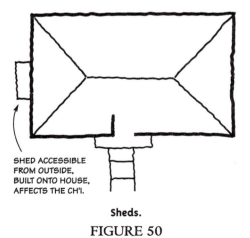

SHED ACCESSIBLE
FROM OUTSIDE,
BUILT ONTO HOUSE,
AFFECTS THE CH'I.

Sheds.

FIGURE 50

makeup alters the look of your face, this addition alters the energy of your house. Notice which gua of the home it falls into and make sure there is nothing hazardous to that particular section's essence. If the family skis are stored neatly in the Family section, there's no problem. If the garbage cans are stored there, you might be looking to rectify this if family matters are priority concerns right now.

How do you treat a detached garage or other outbuildings on the lot?

Whether it's the doghouse or an outhouse, if it is not connected to the building you live in, it is considered a separate feng shui situation (see Figure 51). Place the bagua over it just as you

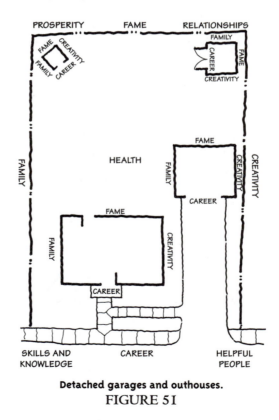

Detached garages and outhouses.
FIGURE 51

did for the house, starting with the door. But one thing you should do is to consider where that outbuilding falls if you overlay the bagua onto the whole lot. You wouldn't want the outhouse in your Prosperity corner. Hey, a toilet is a toilet.

Use the formal entry to the lot as the front door when overlaying the bagua.

Do the closets count as part of the room?

Yes and no. You can use a closet as an addition to the room (like the shed mentioned above) or as a part of it (see Figure 52). Also, if it has a door on it, you can treat it as its own

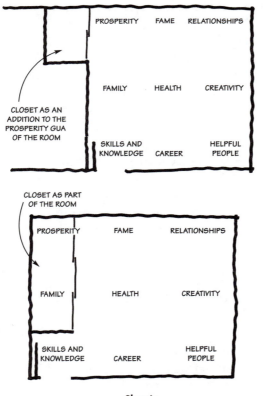

Closets.

FIGURE 52

"room." Just align the bagua of the closet with the closet door and go from there.

I have a sunken living room in the house. Does this affect anything?

Ch'i flows like water. It will eventually flow to the lowest part of the home. If you have a sunken room, counterbalance the flow by placing items anywhere that bring the ch'i back up: mirrors, crystals, ceiling fans, or pictures that have sky, balloons, planes, or birds in them. Or keep the ch'i stirred up with pets, children, and other moving things.

I live in a two-story home with a full basement. Do I feng shui all of the floors?

It is best to review all floors of your home for negative ch'i-flowing conditions and apply proper feng shui cures to them. I'm talking here about things like corners (arrow ch'i) pointing at your bed, beams overhead, and beds in line with doors. But the ground floor—the floor above the basement where the front door is located—is the most important floor to have properly feng shuied.

The other floors should reflect the ground floor's sections of the bagua (either directly above or below it; see Figure 53). If your home is totally unique—say, only the doorway is on one floor, and the rest of the home goes up from there—call a professional or use your intuition as to the best alignment.

My home sits lower than the street. Is that OK?

Yeah, so does mine. This is one of those commonsense ones. Water travels downhill. Street water can now drain toward your house. This is a potential danger. One way to counterbalance this is by symbolically lifting up the rear of the lot and lowering the side adjacent to the street. Place boulders in the front-yard corners to weigh them down, and place "up" lights in the rear corners. Or do whatever else seems appropriate to your situation (see Figure 54).

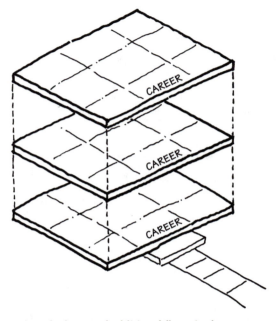

Orient the bagua of additional floors in the same manner as the main floor that includes the front door.

FIGURE 53

I heard it was bad to live in a home sitting at the end of a long street. Is there anything wrong with that?

If you are in line with something like a street (see Figure 55), you may need a little protection. There are several choices. Paint the front door red if it is not out of keeping with your home's decor. If there is a shiny, reflective door knocker on it, so much the better. Hide a mirror in a planter or pot by the front door, facing the street, with the intention of reflecting the street away. Finally, you could place things like boulders in the yard (maybe consult a landscape architect who knows feng shui and other landscape solutions) to slow the ch'i down so it won't hit your home straight on.

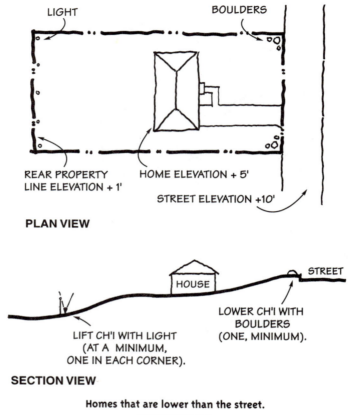

LIGHT   BOULDERS

REAR PROPERTY
LINE ELEVATION + 1'

HOME ELEVATION + 5'

STREET ELEVATION +10'

PLAN VIEW

STREET

HOUSE

LIFT CH'I WITH LIGHT
(AT A MINIMUM,
ONE IN EACH CORNER).

LOWER CH'I WITH
BOULDERS
(ONE, MINIMUM).

SECTION VIEW

Homes that are lower than the street.
FIGURE 54

My home is built on a hillside, and most of the house is on stilts. Is this a problem?

There may be grounding and foundation problems. If you feel as if your head is in the clouds or your feet aren't on the ground, try placing an object of weight (either symbolic weight or actual weight) in the corners of the home that are not touching the ground. Round stones, barbells, or toy heavy machinery can all work with the proper intention. Just place the items in the corner and say to yourself something like, "I am now grounded in my thoughts and actions." (See Figure 56.) Here's

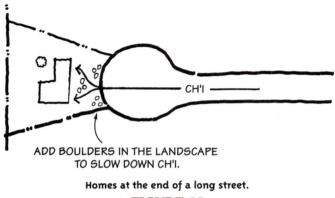

ADD BOULDERS IN THE LANDSCAPE
TO SLOW DOWN CH'I.

Homes at the end of a long street.
FIGURE 55

a personal-grounding cure: place small rounded rocks on top of
a mirror facing up under your bed, in the lower abdomen area.

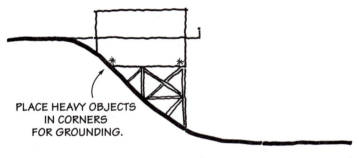

PLACE HEAVY OBJECTS
IN CORNERS
FOR GROUNDING.

Homes on stilts.
FIGURE 56

**My neighbors suck. I want as little to do with them as possible.
Any cures for that?**

Offensive neighbors can make life a wee bit difficult, to say
the least. It's hard to be nurtured by your home if you feel in-
vaded by someone else's noise, smells, junk, or habits. I have two
suggestions. The first is to investigate why you are allowing this
person to rob you of your vital energy. Remember, energy follows thoughts. The more you think about it, the more this clod

is in your life. Perhaps changing your mind would alleviate most of the turmoil. Easier said than done, I know, but I have seen dramatic results with this technique.

My second suggestion would be to use a traditional cure. Place a mirror either on the outside of your house (preferably hidden from view), facing the neighbor, or inside on a wall, still facing the neighbor, and intend for it to reflect all annoyance away from you (see Figure 57). If you are using one outside and have access to one of those Chinese mirrors with the *I Ching* trigrams on it, so much the better (and if you don't know what that is, visit the Web site fengshuipalace.com for more information).

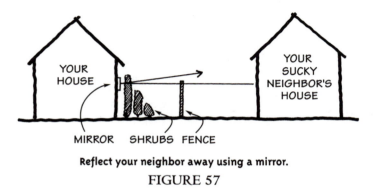

Reflect your neighbor away using a mirror.
FIGURE 57

I recently moved. For some reason I get the creeps whenever I go into one particular room in the house. I think something may have happened in there in the past. Is there anything I can do about that besides avoid the room?

Chances are, if it feels creepy it is creepy. If there are no physical, obvious signs of stagnant ch'i (dead plants, leaky ceilings, grungy walls and furniture), there may be problems on another level (an argument may have occurred there and is still lingering, a death occurred, or the house was built on a burial site). There may even be underground utilities, aquifers, or overhead power lines affecting the space.

There is a rule-of-thumb equation to help you choose the most effective force to use in clearing a space. It is *intensity x duration = force of ch'i*. That means the degree of difficulty in removing the negative ch'i really depends on how long the negativity occurred there and how intense it was. The energy force of a couple quarreling for two months before they divorced and moved out would be different from the energy of a confused teenager who committed suicide in the space. The quarreling couple's energy took longer to create but was not as intense as the suicide.

With any of these situations, space clearing may be necessary. If you don't know exactly what the problem really is, it may be time to call in the professionals. Feng shui consultants (and other professionals such as bau-biologists and dowsers, who scan homes for electromagnetic fields, poor air quality, underground water, and other potentially dangerous items with specific equipment) usually have an arsenal of strategies for handling these conditions.

It is best to apply ritual clearing techniques that equal the force of what you are releasing. For example, spending five minutes with a weak clearing technique in the dead teenager's energy is probably not going to fully release it. I would apply a more intense ritual.

There are many types of effective space clearing rituals out there to use. Whole books are dedicated to the subject. Here is one simple technique that is good for releasing stagnant energy in a room.

First, clean the room. That includes wiping down the walls and touching every surface in the room if you feel it is necessary. Then, peel an orange, making nine pieces of peel in the process. (Set the orange aside.) Place the peels into a dish of fresh water. Clear the room by flicking the water solution around it, using your two middle fingers and thumb (so your hand looks like bull's horns before you flick; see Figure 58). Do this while intending that the room be freed of the stagnant energy. Give thanks when you are done.

If this doesn't do it, I would call in the pros.

Dip your hand into the orange water and then flick the water around the entire room for space clearing.

FIGURE 58

I live on the top floor of a multitenant building. Besides that, the roof above my head is loaded with a bunch of air conditioners and other electrical stuff for the building. Can that be affecting me and my apartment?

Yes, it may be affecting you. The more you are aware of it (sound vibrations when they are turned on, shadows cast over your skylight, cracks in the ceiling), the more it is probably bringing your ch'i down. Use the mirror cure, this time facing up. Intend that it reflect that junk away from you. Work on disguising its physical presence by fixing the cracks and adding a pleasant background sound in your space (like a water feature). See if there's any way to move the item that is casting the shadow.

I live in an apartment above a garage. You said that the ground floor is the most important, so do I have to count the garage as part of my home?

Yes, but deal with it differently.

In general, if your living space is directly above a garage you must take special precautions. Current residential construction practices do little to protect you from the fumes and other negative traits that living above a garage offers (like ch'i whizzing by, in and out all day). Reflect the negative stuff away by using a mirror that faces the problem. That means it is turned facing down in this example. Probably the best location for it is on the floor under a piece of furniture. Place the mirror in this position with that specific intention in mind and you will be protected.

And just like the multitenant dweller, if you live above the ground floor, place something in your home to ground you.

I have a storage room rented somewhere away from my home. Is this a good place to keep my stuff?

It is definitely better than living with it in your home. But it would be better still to not have it at all. Take a good look at the stuff and ask yourself why you are paying to keep it around. Here are some answers that don't fly:

I paid a lot for it.
I might need it in the future.
It was a gift from someone. I can't just get rid of it right away.
It's been in the family for a long time.
I'm afraid to throw anything away.
It might come back in style.

These answers don't fly because they are based either on lack or on guilt. If you come from a point of view of lack, you will never be in the universal flow of things, and yes, things will be hard to come by. And if you have guilt over pitching something, you are living someone else's life and not your own. Is this stuff really worth paying to keep? Think about it.

I live on a houseboat. Can I use feng shui, and if so, how?

If you live in a boat, mobile home, car, or RV, you can still employ feng shui. It is a bit trickier, though, so my best advice would be to call in a professional. But if you are up to it, I would suggest using your intuition as to the bagua layout. Motors usually land in the Fame section, but not always. Start by finding the main door. Use the bagua as usual and see how it feels.

My other suggestion is to be aware of the elements surrounding you and balance them appropriately. Living on so much water in a boat or inside so much metal in an RV can set up ch'i imbalance. Use the Creative and Destructive Cycles described in Chapter I to get into balance.

If you live in a box, tent, cave, or tree house, carry on as usual with the opening as the main doorway, and proceed from there.

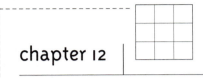

chapter 12

Pump Up the Feng Shui—Adding Extra Power to Your Feng Shui Cures

▼

It's finally time to share the secrets of how to pump up the volume of your feng shui. Once you get the hang of spreading this pixie dust in your home, you will see just how fast your life can really change!

OK, Stuff Moved—Volume Level 3

First of all, by placing the appropriate physical items in the right spot in your home you are on track to achieve success. Let's say, at this rate, your ten-level feng shui power knob is turned up to about level 3. If that is working all right for you, by all means stick with it. Some people can take only a certain amount of change at a time and like to move at a slow pace. Or maybe you have changed only a few things in your home as a tester to see how things go. Fine. As I said before, if it ain't broke, don't fix it. Trust that you will do exactly what you need to do. But if you do want to pump up the feng shui to a higher level, there are several nonphysical things you can do. Using these methods increases the power of your feng shui and lessens the time it takes to achieve results. Are you ready for warp speed?

Before we learn how to pump up the feng shui, please note that in order for you to get from point A to point B in life, some things have to move. Remember, we're talking about making changes here. Some changes may appear negative, but I'll say it again—the universe does not make mistakes. It may look like chaos for a while if you do not like change, but keep the faith— the energy you have put out toward your new goals will make good things happen. If you said you wanted a career change, don't be surprised if you lose your job. If you said you wanted to get along better with your parents, don't be shocked if you have a huge fight with them that exhausts you all into agreeing to see a counselor. Your perception that these things are not good is just that—a perception. They are just what they are, and there is really no good or bad to it until we attach that perception. Keep your focus on the big picture and when these negative things happen, see them as confirmation that you are on the road to getting what you want!

Energy follows thought. So wherever intention goes, the energy flows.

Invisible Feng Shui

Just as we are composed of our physical body and our non-physical mind, feng shui is composed of physical changes (moving your stuff) and changing your mind (with intention). If you think of creating the life changes you want as similar to placing an order in a restaurant, you might better understand what I mean. Picture a restaurant well stocked with the finest ingredients, and you are in the dining room, hungry and looking to place your order. The waiter approaches and says there are no menus because they can make anything—anything. It's up to you to think of exactly what you want. You must get very clear about what you want to eat (just as you must be extremely clear about what you want out of life).

Now, you picture the best meal you can think of, and then you simply state your order. The waiter leaves to tell the chef. You just sit there and wait. That's one way to order. But unfortunately, it is limited by your past dining experiences and your knowledge of food.

Another way is to describe the taste you would like to have, and allow the chef to choose the ingredients he thinks will achieve that sensation. You leave your taste buds in his hands. He may use ingredients you've never heard of or tasted before.

As in the above analogy, there are two ways to place an order. If it is something specific you want, order it. If not, think of the way you want to feel and to be living in the future. Describe it and let the universal chefs cook it up for you. If you are leaving it up to the chefs, I would add cover-your-butt clauses to your request, like "I would like *the perfect* (whatever) for me" or "I would like a new (whatever) *or something better.*" This may help you get the best possible outcome.

The amount of energy you put toward your visualizations, affirmations, and meditations is directly proportional to the results. If you are scattered in your thoughts or do not feel you can make the shifts necessary to counterbalance negative items in the home, it might be wise to call a professional or use the Helpful People visualization in this chapter.

Adding Helpful People to Your Power— Volume Level 5

If you really want to get things moving, get powerful people to help you. Picture this:

Stand in the center of your home and face the Fame section. Then picture some helpful people standing behind you (over your right shoulder) in the Helpful People corner. Now, these other people can be any people you think of as wise and helpful. They can be religious figures like Jesus or Buddha, guardian angels, or your grandmother, who may or may not have passed on. You can even use me as one if you wish (photo on back of book) since I'm trying to be helpful by explaining this wisdom to you in this book. The reason you are doing this is to draw upon their power to help you with giving intention to your new life. Once you have assembled your team, you can proceed to pump up the feng shui knowing that as long as you ask for their help, they indeed will respond.

Reality Bites If You Let It—Volume Level 7

Pump up the feng shui even more using visualization and intention. Those Olympic downhill skiers and divers know the value of visualizing a successful outcome before they compete. They train their minds to see only success, going over their runs and dives in their heads until they believe they can do it and actually feel as if they already did. Tiger Woods said he dreamed of winning the Masters ever since he was a kid. That's about twenty years of visualizing, and his life lined up just perfectly for him to succeed. He was causing his future to happen just as he *thought* it would—so, watch what you think!

When making changes in your home, visualize what you want to have or be in the future. If you are looking for the perfect mate in life, when making adjustments to the Relationship corner visualize yourself already in the perfect relationship. Get into the daydream of it all until you feel yourself crossing over to a place in your mind where you actually feel as if it is already true. The more you can make it feel like the present, the more present it will be. I heard Jim Carrey in an interview say that he used to go up into the Hollywood hills, sit there looking over the valley, and daydream about receiving $10 million for acting services rendered. He said he would not leave the hill until he really believed it was true. To make it more real, he wrote himself a check for $10 million and wrote "acting services rendered" in the memo portion of the check. The check was his physical adjustment to remind him of his goal. He carried the feng shui cure in his wallet! I don't think it was a coincidence that he eventually received exactly $10 million for acting services in one movie deal. How would history have been written about him if every day he had made a point of saying to himself, "I'm never going to make a living acting. Who am I kidding?"

What kind of visualizations should you do? There is really no specific answer, because everyone sees successful results differently. But if you know you want to change something in your life, you probably have already visualized how you want it to be different. Just get in touch with that picture or idea, sit quietly with it, and add power by filling in any missing details. If it is money, fill in the amount and see yourself using it. If it is having your art displayed in an art gallery, picture yourself enjoying the champagne that is being served at the opening. Paint the picture over and over again. Change things if you come up with better ideas. Just keep the thought strong in your mind. Make a habit of consistently going to that place in your mind where the future is real, and you give it even more power.

When you make adjustments to your home, really concentrate on why you are placing an object in a spot. And every time you see the object, it should trigger that future picture in your mind again. It may take a little practice, but it will definitely pump up the feng shui, I'd say to a power level of about 7.

Magic Words—Volume Level 10

Another secret to pumping up the feng shui is to say it out loud. Affirm whatever you want to change in your life. Just as you have visualized the change in your mind, say it in your speech as if it has already been changed. In *Gone with the Wind*, Scarlett O'Hara demonstrated this quite well as she vocalized her vow to the space around her and the dirt in her hand that she would never be hungry again. And remember, anything is possible, so you are limited only by your imagination. Words are filled with a power— power to change your future.

So, when you move your stuff in your house to get results, picture the result you want and declare it out loud as if it has already happened. A great way to do this is to actually give thanks for it as if it has already happened. Say, "Thanks for the money to buy that new house," as you place that little green Monopoly house in your Prosperity corner. And if it is a personal state of being, start it off with an "I am" as if you already are that way. "I am in the perfect relationship with the perfect mate for me." Take some time to come up with your affirmations. The time is well spent. Use adjectives to paint the picture better. Saying, "My backpack purse is totally jammed with cash and all kinds of large checks made out to me!" paints a clearer picture than "I have a lot of money." Both work, but because the first makes you visualize, you are adding more thought to it, thereby giving it more power.

Some important keys to effective affirmations:

- Say, "I am," instead of, "I want," or, "I will" (because if you say, "I want," the universe will keep you wanting it).
- Give thanks as if it has already happened.
- Use adjectives that help make a clear picture.

Here are some generic affirmations for each area of the bagua. You can use them as is, or build up your own picture by adding your personal meaningful adjectives to them.

Family

I feel great and I am in perfect health.
I find joy in my family relationships.
I find strength in my flexibility with others.
People always treat me like part of their family.

Prosperity

Money finds me easily, now and always.
I always have enough money.
As I give to others, I receive.

Fame
I am well respected in the world.
I am well known for my talents and skills.

Relationships
I am in the perfect loving, intimate relationship.
I accept myself unconditionally and love and honor myself.
I love everyone, and receive love from everyone.

Creativity
I find joy in my ability to easily express my creativity.
There is an endless supply of creative talent within me, and I
  am able to tap into it whenever I wish.
I am in perfect harmony and balance with my children.

Helpful People
I am always in the right place at the right time.
People are always available to help when I need them.
People always treat me fairly and honestly.

Career
I am now living my true calling.
I am now in the flow of my destiny.
I now live the perfect life for me.
The universe now knows my dreams and is making it my
  reality.

Skills and Knowledge
I am a wise person in all situations.
The genius within me is now available and I am in touch with
  universal wisdom.

Health
I feel great and I am in perfect health.
I am centered, grounded, healthy, and at peace with all.
I am harmonious and find joy in my own power.
Joyful surprises reach me every day.

If you do not wish to say an affirmation, you can give power with your speech by saying what the Tibetan monks call the six true words. They are *Om ma ni pad me hum* (pronounced *aum, ma, nee, paad, mee, hum*).

There is a long story as to what they mean and why they are used, but they still work without your knowing all about that (kind of like how people say *"Gesundheit!"* when someone sneezes—what the heck does that mean?). Just say these words out loud (and I would recommend saying them nine times) after visualizing your result in each area of the bagua. No religious conversion needed.

If the whole affirmation thing is not your scene, try simply giving thanks. You can thank the people who have given you the stuff that you just moved around, you can thank the people who allowed you to make the money to buy the stuff, or you can thank God or the universe for providing these things. Or finally, you can thank your lucky stars for finding this information so you can create more opportunities to give thanks.

Walk the Walk and Talk the Talk— Volume Level 12

If you do your visualizations and affirmations in a specific order, you can add yet another level of power. In feng shui terms, it is called *tracing the nine stars.* (Each "star" is one of the areas of the bagua.) Employing all of the above techniques to your cures will increase your feng shui power exponentially to around level 12 on your ten-level volume knob.

Start in the Family gua by literally going there, standing, perhaps touching one of the items you placed there, and then doing your visualizations and affirmations. Continue doing the same thing in all of the other areas. Follow this order: (1) Family, (2) Prosperity, (3) Health, (4) Helpful People, (5) Creativity, (6) Skills and Knowledge, (7) Fame, (8) Career, (9) Relationships. (See Figure 59.)

Don't worry if prohibiting walls fall in your path and make

you enter an out-of-order gua on your way to the correct one. It will work anyway.

When to Call In the Pros

Since this book is confined to describing the very basic principles of feng shui, it may be in your best interest to seek the advice and counsel of a feng shui professional in certain circumstances. Extreme physical or mental health conditions, physically dangerous situations, and cases of haunting are better left to professionals.

There are several styles of feng shui. Make sure you are comfortable with the style the practitioner uses. Ask them what style they practice when interviewing them.

If you have your home set up based upon this book and would like to find someone that practices close to this style, I

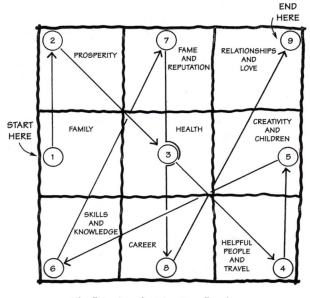

The "Tracing the Nine Stars" order.

FIGURE 59

OK, I Moved My Stuff—Has My Life Changed Yet?

I wanted to make this final note hit home with the power it deserves. The answer to the question above is undoubtedly *yes*. Your life has changed because you have *willed* it to. Everything you do affects your future, so by merely reading this book (even without moving your stuff) you have ever so slightly propelled yourself further along your path in an ever so slightly different direction. When you project that slight change in course far into the future, you will obviously arrive at a place that is very far from the original fork in the road. The more you intend to make change, the more off your old path you will be.

The fact that human beings have free will is an essential ingredient in the workings of feng shui. Because the future can be changed, and this change is guided by our thoughts, we can discover ways to use the universal power to create our vision of the perfect future. This may include a loving relationship, material wealth, or a host of other awesome events and circumstances. Your intention matters because of the energy it is constantly pulling toward you. If you notice, those who constantly harp on the negative are usually surrounded by it. And those who always seem to see the good in things more often find themselves in rosy situations. And let's not forget the ambivalent ones out there, who do not focus on anything in particular and wonder why nothing ever really happens in their lives worth talking about. They probably wouldn't recognize their life path if it had a neon sign pointing toward it! Your thoughts are of great importance, and they *matter*. Notice the word *matter*? Your thoughts create matter. It is this matter that you are striving to bring about and change with feng shui. Thoughts control matter—therefore your intentions are a key ingredient in feng shui. Give something mundane an intention, and its matter will change. Common laws of physics have proven this. You affect even those things that you breeze by without the slightest notice. So imagine what happens if you actually give notice. Take charge of your life by evaluating what things are working for you now and what things need to be upgraded in order to do so. Find a love source inside, bring it forth, and guide it toward higher thoughts.

As souls playing humans for a time on this planet, we have been given one gift that allows us to change paths the very instant we choose to change our minds—the gift of free will. It is the most awesome gift because we are bound by nothing but our own imagination.

I have often described the path that got me to where I am as quite rocky and filled with burdens. But I take the responsibility for choosing to see the path that way. The reality is, they were merely events. I added the negative perception to them with my free will. Yet as everyone always says, if those events didn't happen, I wouldn't be who I am—so I wouldn't want to change a thing.

If you must, look at your total past as merely one big character-building lesson. Now that you know how to change your future life by simply moving your stuff and intending your ultimate future to be so, look at your future as one big unwritten chapter filled with everything you can think of—*and take responsibility for it.*

So remember, be careful, and always be aware of what you are thinking—and have a great life!

If you would like additional feng shui information, or products used for cures—or to air your comments about this book—please visit my Web site:
http://www.fengshuipalace.com